War Child

Adverse Childhood Experiences, Combat Trauma, and the Search for Peace.

Anthony Jacks

ISBN: 979-8-9933689-0-0
First Edition

Content Note
This book contains descriptions of **child abuse, suicidal ideation, and graphic combat violence**. Reader discretion advised.

If you are in crisis, in the U.S. you can call or text **988** (Suicide & Crisis Lifeline) or visit **988lifeline.org**. Veterans can press **1** after dialing or text **838255**.

Disclaimer: This book is a work of personal experience and reflection. It is not intended as medical or psychological advice. Readers dealing with trauma, mental health challenges, or suicidal thoughts are encouraged to seek professional support.

TABLE OF CONTENTS

"Tell me, Muse, of the man of many turns, who wandered many ways after the fall of Troy, who saw the cities of many men and suffered many woes upon the sea."

— Homer, *The Odyssey*, Book I, A.T. Murray trans. (1919, public domain, adapted)

Prologue: The War Within

The War for The Mind

The line at the gas station moved slow enough for my mind to wander. Two spots ahead, a couple who looked like they'd slept in their car whispered over lottery numbers. The clerk, a big Indian guy—dot, not feather—waited for them with the kind of patience only boredom can teach. Right in front of me, a woman squeezed her daughter's hand like she was keeping them both tethered to earth.

The speaker in the ceiling changed songs and a drum beat cut through the fluorescent hum. I didn't expect to know the words. But the voice came in anyway.

Somebody Told Me, The Killers.

I hadn't listened to them in years. Not that song. Not since Steel Curtain.

Major Mendoza's face lived in my head like a still frame: huge, broad-shouldered, a man who could throw lieutenants like straw men and still make them stand straighter for it. He'd given the best precombat speech I ever heard—no bullshit, no false comforts, just a clean argument for courage. His men loved him.

In Ubaydi, he stepped on a pressure plate, connected to two 155's. The biggest pieces of his body that they could find, were his hands. The hands I had watched him take on all comers with.

The woman in front of me turned while I was staring past her. Our eyes met for a flash, and she looked away. Whenever that happens, I wonder if people can see that I am haunted.

I handed my cash over—"sixty on three, please"—and thought about control. The system that runs my life is little more than ledger lines and micromanagement: show up, clock in, don't fall through the cracks where people disappear. My worry this morning was ordinary—how to make rent, how to keep myself above the bottom.

I pushed the glass door open. Midday heat, radiating in waves off the blacktop. The speakers outside bumped up the volume. Mendoza's men chose this song for a memorial video that senior enlisted staff made. When I saw it, I knew that I would never be able to listen to that song again without remembering.

Across the lane, a jacked-up Dodge took a fuel pump from a cowboy whose rear window sticker said MOLON LABE like it was a personality. On the other side, a Subaru sat with a rainbow charm swaying from the mirror; the driver's lavender hair caught the breeze as she hunched over her phone.

Two tribes fueling up, side by side: the armor and the ornament. I thought about the shouting on cable TV, the pundits turning outrage into quarterly growth, the podcasts promising apocalypse. Up close, though, I watched people buy brands and slogans the same way ancient folk bought charms—because belonging looks like protection.

It's all tribal instinct—an ancient survival reflex—rewired and repackaged to keep us divided. The machine doesn't care which flag you wave, only that you wave it hard enough to forget the person across the pump is built just like you.

When I'd finished fueling, I got back in the truck. Stella — my bird dog — stuck her head up and nuzzled my hand off the gear shift and onto her head. She doesn't care about tribes or pundits. She knows only the ledger we can see: food, walk, sun. Today, we are going hunting, her favorite.

This is the war I live in now—less about lines on a map than about the slow business of control: who gets to decide what is safe, what counts as truth, and who is allowed to belong. It's the war for the mind, for your obedience. Because what feels ordinary on the surface—gas stations, grocery aisles, paychecks—hides the deeper conflict.

The War Today

Veterans return home from wars with bullets and bombs into a war they can't name—one fought not with shooting, but with debt, division, and despair. We are told it is peace, yet it consumes our time, our labor, our souls. It is the same war we were raised inside without knowing it: a culture that confuses captivity for accomplishment and silence for strength.

Coming home can feel harder than going to war. Survival in battle doesn't guarantee peace afterward, and too many of us return carrying shame, guilt, rage, and despair that have no easy name. This book is my attempt to map those hidden wounds. I can't promise neat answers, but I can tell the truth as I've lived it. It is also a record of the small, unruly moments that say, *I'm still alive*—the laugh no one expects from a man who just walked out of the fire.

This book is a field journal from the war after the war. And it begins long before enlistment. Many of us were wounded as children—abused, neglected, abandoned. We brought those injuries with us into the military, where we found structure, identity, and a kind of meaning.

But war doesn't just resurrect old wounds—it forges new ones. It turns survival mechanisms into weapons. It fuses early trauma with battlefield trauma until the soul can no longer tell where one ends and the other begins.

Many of us were carrying wounds older than ourselves—pain handed down like heirlooms, shaping our minds before we had the chance to choose who we would become.

This book is not just about PTSD or TBI or moral injury—though we will talk about all of those things. It's about what happens when a man is torn between who he was raised to be, who he became in war, and who he is now, trying to survive in a world that has no idea what he's lived through.

Like Odysseus, we return home in pieces. Changed. Disoriented. Sometimes dishonest. Sometimes dangerous. But also carrying wisdom—hard-earned truths that could help others if only we knew how to share them. If only we were given the space to speak.

This is my space to speak. And maybe, it will be yours too.

If you are a veteran, this book is for you. Not as therapy, but as truth. If you are someone who loves a veteran, this book is for you—because you deserve to understand what they may never fully be able to say. And if you are a counselor, policymaker, or citizen who cares about the moral fabric of this nation, then this book is for you too—because our wounds are not just personal. They are national. And ignoring them will cost us all.

The Ancient War

Long before bullets and blast waves, long before the dusty streets of Fallujah or the mud-walled villages of Afghanistan, there was Troy. There was Achilles—godlike, invincible, wrathful—brought to his knees not by spears or arrows, but by grief. His best friend, Patroclus, died because of a command decision he failed to prevent. In his rage, Achilles became something less than human—and when the fighting was done, he sat alone in the dust, consumed by what he had done, and by what he had lost.

The war within the souls of men is older than history. Homer knew this. The *Iliad* and the *Odyssey* were never just about strategy or conquest—they were about what war does to a man. How it breaks him open. How it steals his identity. How it tempts him with glory, then abandons him in grief. And how, if he survives, he wanders not only across seas but across years of inner ruin, trying to find his way back home.

That ancient war still rages today—in the minds of combat veterans, in the broken marriages and sleepless nights, in the silent rooms where men stare down the barrel of a gun not because they want to die, but because they don't know how to live anymore.

A Prayer Across Ages

These wounds are not just private sorrows; they are threads in the larger fabric of our culture. If we don't face them, they don't disappear—they spread.

The war within does not end with a ceasefire. It does not end when the medals are handed out or the flag is folded. It ends—or begins to end—only when we understand what it means to lose that war: to give up on life, to vanish in shame, to go unheard. When we start speaking the truth about what happened. When we refuse to be silent. When we seek not just to survive, but to be made whole again—not who we were, but something wiser, stronger.

This is not an indictment. It is a testament.
A roadmap drawn in scar tissue.
A signal fire lit in the dark.
And a prayer whispered across the ages—from Achilles to now:

May you fight on.
May you find your way home.
May you live.

Part I: Wired for Survival
Building a Warrior from a Child

"But no man hath ever escaped his fate, be he coward or brave, once he hath been born."

— Homer, *The Iliad*, Book VI, trans. A.T. Murray, 1924 (public domain)

Chapter 1: The First Battlefield

How Early Wounds Built My Armor

"The wretched race, forever prey to pain and grief."

— Homer, *The Iliad*, Book XVIII, trans. Alexander Pope, 1715
(public domain, adapted)

The First Battlefield

The first battlefield I ever fought on wasn't in Iraq or Afghanistan. It was in my childhood home.

My mother had a hair-trigger temper and a kind of chaos around her that could shift the atmosphere in a room before she even spoke. You could feel her moods the same way you feel the weather breaking before a thunderstorm.

Early on, I learned that silence could be safety and compliance could buy peace, but I also knew I resented those lessons. My brothers and I were taught to disappear when the screaming started. We became shadows in our own home.

I don't remember moments of comfort or affection. What I remember is the watching. The way we tracked her every movement, every shift in her breathing, like animals sensing a storm. We listened for the sharp change in her tone, the clipped edge that meant the air was about to crack. Even laughter could be dangerous—it could flip without warning into rage.

My body lived on a hair trigger. My shoulders rose, my stomach knotted, my breath went shallow at the faintest flicker of anger in her face. I would shrink inside myself, hoping to become invisible, to not give her anything to strike at. It was like standing on the edge of a cliff, waiting for the ground to crumble.

I remember the way fear hollowed me out, made me weightless, like disappearing might be the only safe thing left to do.

I remember the night she snatched me off my feet and hurled me into the yard. I was in my underwear. There was snow on the ground, sharp as broken glass against my bare skin. The door slammed behind me, the lock clicking like the snap of a trap.

I pounded my fists against the door until they went numb. Inside, the house was warm and golden, shadows moving behind the curtains. I stood there shivering, teeth rattling, not sure if she would ever let me back in.

Eventually, my brothers cracked open the man door to the garage and whispered out, their faces pale with fear—as if rescuing me might get them thrown out too.

I didn't know it at the time, but I was already experiencing what would later be classified as complex trauma. I wasn't just reacting to my environment—I was being rewired by it. The hypervigilance, the insomnia, the sense of never feeling safe or good enough—these weren't things I developed after combat. They were things I brought with me to the battlefield.

This was not just personal pain—it was part of something older, passed from parent to child like an heirloom of fear. What I carried into war had been carried into me.

My nervous system was trained to anticipate betrayal, to scan for danger, to strike before being struck. This wiring served me well in war, but it sabotaged me in every other setting.

Even as a teenager, long before I wore a uniform, I carried this war inside. My emotions swung between numbness and rage. I couldn't trust anyone deeply, not even those closest to me. And I couldn't trust myself—my needs, my longings, my sense of worth. What looked like independence was often just dissociation. My childhood hadn't just damaged me—it had drafted me into a lifelong fight to prove I wasn't broken.

What I remember of my childhood is full of screaming, violence, and abandonment. My mother, a career nurse with eyes as cold and hard as surgical steel, made it brutally clear: we—my father, my two brothers, and I—were an inconvenience, a festering wound on her meticulously crafted life.

Motherhood? A loathsome shackle.
Housewifery? An unspeakable prison.

Those few years my father managed to coax her home were a scorched-earth campaign of misery. A low, simmering depression, laced with sudden, explosive violence, pulsed through our lives.

A flash of white knuckles, her fist and forearm hitting me in my upheld guard—not a mere slap, but a calculated blow with enough force to send me sprawling. As I tried to get back to my feet, she used her heel to knock me flat again. This was her dance of humiliation. The bitter tang of tears, the choked sobs forced from my throat, were the only music that satisfied her.

She wanted to break us—to extinguish the flickering flame of our spirits.

As adolescence approached, I started to push back, only to be labeled the aggressor, the violent one—a monster in her distorted narrative. They took me to a mental hospital, where I was diagnosed with anger issues and depression.

No one asked what had been done to me. They only asked what was wrong with me.

The psychologist never even spoke to me. He spoke to my mother and father on the far side of the room while I sat in a plastic chair, watching them talk about me as if I weren't there. I remember the sight of them glancing over at me, the hum of fluorescent lights, the way my feet didn't quite touch the floor.

My mother's voice was sharp and certain. My father said almost nothing, just nodded along with whatever she said. I could see the fear in the way he avoided her eyes. He was just as scared of her as we were.

At just twelve years old, I was prescribed Wellbutrin. The medication dulled everything. It was like living underwater—no joy, no fear, no anger, just the distant echo of who I had been.

Looking back, I see that this was my first taste of the invisible war— the way our systems protect themselves by silencing the wounded instead of listening to them.

In the clinic, I don't know what anyone could have said to make a difference. I didn't see any way out of it for me then, and looking back on it, I still don't. It's like the path was meant for me, and there was nothing but to endure. Even as a child I felt that way. When the pain felt like it was going to crush me, I would contemplate suicide, cut myself, and chain-smoke cigarettes.

Exile and Escape

I stayed on the medication until I was sent to spend the summer with my uncle. What the pills flattened, the summer stretched: hours of quiet where I realized numbness wasn't the same thing as peace.

He left me mostly to myself. I spent most of the summer fishing for crappie and catching crawdads in the local pond, the sun hot on my shoulders, dragonflies skimming the water like living sparks. I was alone most of the time.

I remember finding *Debbie Does Dallas* in the drawer of the TV cabinet—my first time seeing pornography. Not exactly a lesson about love. Just another example of growing up without any real guidance, learning about sex from a movie about a woman who prostitutes herself to afford a cheerleading trip.

After I came back home, I found marijuana with my friends.

The first time I felt marijuana, I was sitting beside a small lake in my friend's little Bronco II.
We passed a joint back and forth, the sweet smoke curling through the cracked windows. I remember feeling a sudden rush of excitement—and then something else entirely.
Stillness.

The world seemed to open up around me, the sunlight soft on the water, the ripples turning to liquid glass. For the first time I could remember, my body felt calm, like I wasn't bracing for impact. I didn't want to go anywhere. I just wanted to stay there.

It was the opposite of everything I had ever known—and I think that's why it sank its hooks in so deep.

It numbed the sharp edges my mother had carved into me. It became my way of disappearing without having to leave.

My teenage years were a blur of juvenile probation, the soul-crushing monotony of work programs, and long hours spent drawing in detention halls. All the while, the festering wound of my childhood grew. My mother was working nights in the city. She'd disappear for days, sometimes weeks, spending her days at her friends' or in motel rooms.

In detention hall, I would sit hunched over the scarred wooden desk, the smell of pencil shavings and old floor wax heavy in the air. The fluorescent lights humming and flickering in the windowless room, illuminating the graphite smudges covering my hands.

I drew horrible pictures—grotesque, surreal things. Twisted, broken bodies. Scenes of battle and torture. I don't know where those images came from or why they fascinated me, only that they poured out of me as if they'd been waiting.

Maybe I was exorcising something. Maybe I was giving shape to a pain I didn't have words for.

While I drew, the noise of the world faded. The weight lifted for a little while, and I could almost breathe.

I read constantly back then, as I still do, always carrying a book around. One day I'd fallen asleep in math class, my head pillowed on an old black hardback with red lettering. The room was hushed, chalk dust drifting in the slanting light.

I woke to a sudden jolt—my head bouncing off the desk as the book was pulled from under me. I wiped the drool from my cheek and blinked up to see my teacher standing over me. She was staring at the title on the cover.

Paradise Lost, Milton.

Her face shifted from irritation to something like wonder. Without a word, she handed the book back to me and walked away, shaking her head slightly. It was as if she'd decided in that instant to stop trying to understand me—and just leave me alone.

Looking back, I think I was already trying to escape—not just the classroom, but the world I'd been handed.

No one knew what to do with kids like me.
Wounded boys don't fit the lesson plan, so the system either tries to fix us—or forget us.

More than anything else, I escaped into books.
While art was how I bled out what was inside me, reading was how I slipped free of it altogether.

My grandma had read with me when I was just three or four, her voice patient and warm, guiding my finger under the words. By eleven, I was reading *Moby-Dick* and other classics no one expected me to understand.

Reading was the greatest gift I ever received. It lit a path out of the chaos—and it's that same love of books that lets me tell this story now.

By seventeen, art had become the only part of me I still believed in. While everything else about me felt broken, drawing made me feel real.

One night I painted a mural across my bedroom wall—my name, ANTHONY, in block letters dripping blood and flickering with painted flames, a three-dimensional illusion that seemed to jump off the wall. It felt like claiming space in a world where I was supposed to be invisible.

But in my mother's eyes, it was rebellion. An act of defiance she couldn't control.

She called the sheriff. I watched from the hallway as the deputy stood stiffly beside her, the cold, impersonal weight of the law behind him, while she signed the paperwork that made me a trespasser in my own home.

He walked me out like I was being evicted from a place I had never truly been allowed to belong. She got a restraining order. When I left home, I told myself it was freedom.
In truth, it was just another exile.

After the mural incident, I went to live with an older friend on the nearby Indian reservation—not exactly the safest place for a white boy.

My friend was Native enough to get a house and government commodities, and he let me stay in a spare room on a stained old mattress. He fed me from his groceries, never asking for anything in return.

He sold drugs. The house was strung with death metal posters, satanic symbols, and torn pages of pornography pinned like trophies to the walls. But it was quieter than the house I'd come from.

No screaming.
No sudden violence.
Just the low hum of guitars through blown-out speakers and the occasional clink of a lighter.

Even while I lived on the reservation, I couldn't fully cut the cord. When my mother was away, I'd slip back to the old house to check on my father.

The place felt strange without her—as if she had exerted so much control to claim it all for herself, only to abandon it like it had never mattered at all. The air seemed hollow yet heavy, like the walls remembered her even when she wasn't there.

My Father's Decline

And my father…
his slow, agonizing descent into Alzheimer's had begun when I was twelve. By seventeen, he was a stranger, a broken man, haunted by shadows only he could see.

One night, during a small gathering while Mom was away, my father walked into the room completely naked.

At first I just stared, stunned. His pale body looked thin, except for his potbelly, his shoulders sagging under some invisible weight. Then the blue metallic glint caught my eye—a .357 Magnum clutched in his right hand.

Time fractured.

He raised the pistol and swept it across the room in a wild arc, his arm trembling. That was when the fear hit.

His eyes were cloudy, vacant, like he was searching for ghosts. His chest heaved. Spittle clung to his lip.

He didn't recognize me.

His voice came out as a slurred snarl, thick with rage and confusion, ordering us to get out, to flee his shattered kingdom. The words didn't make sense, but the gun did.

I knew better than to move toward him.
I raised my hands slowly, palms out, keeping my voice calm, steady— anything to hold his attention. My heart was pounding, but my face stayed still.

Behind me, I heard the shuffle of feet as the other kids slipped toward the door. No one spoke. No one dared.

I stood there as the last of them escaped, his wild eyes locked on me, until I finally backed away too—slowly, never turning my back, slipping through the doorway and pulling it shut behind me.

The weight didn't hit me until I was outside, gulping cold night air like I'd just surfaced from underwater.
He hadn't just forgotten who I was.
He had forgotten he loved me.

That night didn't just frighten me—it humiliated me.
It was more of the same, really: another lesson in disappointment.

I had always identified myself with my father, as I think all children do.
He was supposed to be my anchor, my proof that I came from something solid.

Seeing him like that—naked, lost, waving a gun at strangers—filled me with a shame I didn't have words for. It felt like watching my future unravel in front of me.

Somewhere deep down, I think that was the moment I stopped looking for myself in him—and started searching for who I was somewhere else.

In the years that followed, my father unraveled slowly, thread by thread.

At first it was little things—misplacing his keys, forgetting appointments. Then whole conversations began to disappear from his memory as if they'd been erased. I'd answer the same question three times in an hour, watching the confusion knot his brow each time like it was brand new.

By seventeen, he was a ghost in his own house. He shuffled through the rooms in loose pajamas, muttering to people who weren't there. Sometimes I would find him standing at the window for hours, staring into the yard as if waiting for something only he could see.

At other times, his confusion turned violent. He became convinced that my mother was an imposter.

He would seize her by the upper arms with his vise-grip hands and shake her, demanding to know what she had done with his wife. Her arms were often mottled with dark bruises from these outbursts.

The man who had once been the quiet center of our family was dissolving, and no one came to help.

I could see the fear in her too—the way she left for longer and longer stretches, as if she could outrun what was happening to him.

I didn't know it then, but I do now: prolonged psychological stress can ravage the brain. The hippocampus, which governs memory, is especially vulnerable to the flood of cortisol that chronic stress unleashes (Mason et al., 2001). My father lived under relentless pressure—marriage, money, a house thick with conflict—and his mind simply couldn't hold together under it.

His life was a heartbreaking paradox. He wanted peace, just a quiet cabin in the woods, but he was trapped in a war he could never name.

And I watched him disappear, piece by piece.

There's something uniquely shattering about watching the person you come from come apart. I felt like I was losing my father, but also losing part of myself—my history, my roots, my proof that I belonged to something.

It taught me a brutal lesson: if I wanted to survive, I couldn't depend on anyone else to hold me together.

My father, personally, was a mystery to me. He never talked about himself or told us stories.

When I was seven years old, he took me camping and taught me how to shoot a rifle. He used the same precise, no-nonsense methods his father had used with him—both had been competitive marksmen. He showed me how to line up the sights, control my breathing, squeeze the trigger, and follow through.

For a few hours, he seemed almost proud of me. It's incredible how far in life that single lesson carried me—the only thing I can clearly say I learned from him.

Even that lesson felt less like connection than obligation—as if he was passing down a skill because it was expected, not because he wanted to share a piece of himself. I think much of his parenting, even the choice to have children at all, was shaped by what the world expected of him—not by any real desire to love and nurture young boys.

I suspect he thought my mother would give us that love.
And I think he lived in quiet anguish after realizing she never would.

When I was eleven, I made the mistake of muttering an obscenity about my mother while she was in the middle of humiliating me at the dinner table.

He didn't say a word. He just hit me.

A single punch to the side of my face. I never saw it coming.

I woke up on the kitchen floor, drooling on the rug, my head ringing. He was still seated at the table, looking down at me with a cold, unreadable expression.

There were no lectures, no lessons—just the message that defiance would be met with force.

I picked myself up and walked to my room in silence.

Looking back, it's hard to separate those two memories—the rifle and the fist.

They were nothing alike, yet somehow, they fused in my mind as proof that love was supposed to hurt, and that strength was the only way to be seen.

Anger lived under my skin like a simmering pot, always threatening to boil over.
I knew it was unhealthy, destructive even, but it was familiar, and I had yet to find a way to be at peace without it.

Only years later did I understand where that anger came from.
It wasn't just personality. It was wiring.

The Adverse Childhood Experiences Study—ACEs for short—looks
at how childhood trauma shapes health and behavior across a
lifetime.

The results are devastating. Children who experience abuse, neglect,
or household dysfunction are significantly more likely to suffer from
depression, substance abuse, heart disease, and even early death
(Felitti et al., 1998).

When I take this test honestly, without minimizing what I can
remember, I score 7 out of 10.
A score of 4/10 is considered high risk for the physical and
psychological problems listed above.

It was sobering to see my childhood reduced to checkboxes… and to
see how directly it mapped onto the person I had become.

One thing I wish someone had told me early in life:

Do not compare your experiences of pain with that of another.

There's always someone who has it worse than you.

I learned that firsthand during my time in Kabul in 2017, working in
two-man teams in unmarked vehicles and plainclothes I witnessed
the plight of the street children, thousands of orphans created by the
bombs.

One evening, stuck in traffic, a begging boy reached my car.
He put his hands against my window, using them to cut the glare and
peer in.

First, he looked at me—shaved head, glasses, bushy beard.
Then his eyes shifted to my partner sitting shotgun.

His reaction to my partner's shaved face and bleach-blonde
mohawk—a screaming, distraught display—revealed a horrifying
truth: the boy believed we'd killed his family.
Bombs had fallen from the sky, and then he was alone.

At first, I didn't understand his screams or frantic pantomimes.
Hands up to the sky and then falling to the ground, crying and
slapping my window with his palms.
All I could think was that we were compromised and that his
emotional outburst was going to draw attention.

My Green Beret colleague, who had worked extensively with
Afghans, calmly explained what the boy was saying—without ever
looking over at him.

For twenty minutes, trapped in a sea of witnesses, I felt the weight of
his accusation and the immense sorrow of a child's loss.

Compared to his suffering, my own problems seemed insignificant. It
was through the analysis of my thoughts about the street children
that I came to realize that I had been taught to dismiss my own pain.

I had learned to inflict suffering on myself—a voice of relentless self-
deprecation that invalidated my emotions and convinced me of my
insignificance.
My joy, my anguish, my very essence—none of it felt like it mattered.

This destructive pattern came from a single habit: measuring my
worth against others.

I would pinpoint my own distress, then cruelly contrast it with the suffering of others, silencing myself with the lie that my pain was not enough to count, that someone else had it worse.

I learned that voice from my mother.
And she learned it from hers.
And so on.

Realizing that doesn't silence the voice.
But it helped me see it wasn't the truth—it was just old wiring.

My journey of healing has been long and uneven. It has meant learning to sit with memories I once buried, to let myself feel what I trained myself not to feel.

It has meant reshaping my nervous system one breath at a time— teaching my body it is safe when it does not believe it, offering myself compassion when the old voice tells me I don't deserve it.

It has also meant drawing boundaries so sharp they sometimes cut— keeping distance from my mother, protecting the fragile pieces of self I am still rebuilding.
The work has been grueling, but with the help of therapy and the support of my brother, I have made real progress.

I am learning to live a life not dictated by the wounds of my past.

And yet, the road is never straight.
There are still days when the little boy inside me feels lost and small.
On those days, I am learning to be gentle with him—to give myself the comfort and protection I never received.

Armor and Achilles

It is in that shared fire that I've come to understand Achilles
differently… his rage, his despair, his fury.

The greatest of the Greeks was not just grieving for Patroclus, nor
simply venting frustration at Agamemnon's greed or dishonor.
His rage came from deeper wounds, from pain he could not name.
He was fighting a war within as much as a war without, wrestling
with the invisible ghosts that haunt all men: shame, loss,
abandonment, betrayal.

Like Achilles, I carried those ghosts onto every battlefield I ever
faced.

Homer's words, stark and unyielding, echo through the centuries
because they speak an uncomfortable truth: we men—especially
those forged in violent fires—are indeed wretched things.
Not wretched in weakness, but in the unseen suffering we hide
behind our armor.

This armor is not made of bronze or iron but of scars and silence,
forged in the earliest conflicts we endure.

For me, it was childhood, not combat, that first taught me to armor
myself—to bury emotion beneath readiness, to hide vulnerability
behind defiance, to guard intimacy with suspicion.

My mother's rage and my father's distant silence were the first blows
in a lifelong battle to prove I was not broken.

Yet the harder I fought, the deeper I reinforced the very trauma I
sought to escape.
Each punch thrown, every act of youthful rebellion, every violent

outburst was another attempt to reclaim a sense of power that had been stolen from me as a child.

Like Achilles, whose grief transformed into unrelenting fury, my rage was not strength—it was survival.

It was desperation masquerading as defiance.

My nervous system, trained early to anticipate betrayal and threat, became a relentless sentry—always on guard, never at ease. Like Achilles standing at the ramparts, watching for the Trojans' next assault, I watched for signs of emotional ambush from lovers, friends, even family.

In relationships, my hypervigilance didn't look like strength—it looked like distance.
What I believed was composure was really dissociation.
What I called independence was often just isolation.

My emotional withdrawal wasn't seen as stoicism but as indifference.
The women I loved could feel it, even when I couldn't name it.
I wasn't being strong; I was bracing.

Bracing for the blow that never came, but that I always expected.

That is what living in armor does.
It doesn't just keep the world out—it keeps you locked inside.

And yet, it wasn't only fear and vigilance that my childhood instilled in me.
There was also resilience—an ability to endure, to survive repeated blows and still rise to fight again.

Homer's heroes are not just warriors; they are survivors.
They bear wounds that do not always bleed, but ache deeply, invisibly.

Achilles wore his grief openly, tearing his hair, mourning in agony, unable to hide his inner torment.

I too, carried wounds I could neither name nor fully heal.

Unlike Achilles, I hid my grief beneath layers of denial and self-destruction.
Only now do I recognize how profoundly my childhood prepared me for combat—not because it taught me bravery, but because it taught me to live in constant readiness for betrayal, pain, and loss.

Achilles was driven by unconscious forces—grief, rage, fear—that shaped his destiny, leading inevitably toward destruction.

By beginning to confront my own unconscious trauma, I took the first steps away from a fate of repetition and toward true healing.

The work is slow, painful, and imperfect.
But each step forward is a step away from unconscious suffering.

I once believed the armor I wore—crafted from childhood wounds and adolescent defiance—made me strong. But I see now: true strength is not found in the armor we build to protect ourselves, but in our willingness to take it off.

Achilles' tragedy was not his vulnerability—it was his refusal to lay down the armor until it was too late. The hero who could conquer armies could not conquer himself.

We men, as Homer reminds us, are indeed wretched things—
wretched not because we are weak, but because we deny our wounds,
hide our scars, and mistake hardness for healing.

My first battlefield taught me to survive but not how to live.
It gave me armor, but took away my capacity for trust, intimacy, and
peace.

Only now, in the slow work of honesty, am I discovering what lies
beneath the armor:
a wounded, vulnerable, deeply human heart.

I am beginning to understand that my childhood did not only build
my armor; it forged my compassion too.

In acknowledging my wounds, I am learning to see and honor the
wounds of others.
My pain has become a bridge, a point of connection, rather than a
fortress.

Perhaps the truest courage is not that of Achilles, charging heroically
into battle,
but the quieter bravery required to face our inner wounds—
the courage to be vulnerable, to be known, and to finally lay down
our armor.

Chapter 2: Trauma as a Foundation

Early Scars, Lifelong Battles

"The gods have spun the thread for mortals, that they must live in pain, while the gods themselves are sorrowless."

— Homer, *The Iliad*, Book XXIV, public domain translation (adapted)

Why the Military

Childhood trauma is not something we leave behind with age; it becomes the architecture of our inner world. For those who grow up in environments marked by fear, abandonment, or abuse, identity doesn't form in the warm light of love but in the cold shadow of survival. The emotional damage inflicted in youth is often masked by grit, defiance, or a relentless work ethic—tools for endurance, not healing. For some of us, the military feels like a lifeline, not just because of its stability or honor, but because it mirrors the conditions we've already been forced to survive.

A profound self-doubt and a desperate need for validation propelled me toward military life. I craved the power, the lethal potential, a visceral yearning to prove my worth – not just to others, but to myself. This hunger for self-defense masked a darker impulse, a destructive force I struggled to contain. My chaotic existence, a relentless cycle of dead-end jobs and crushing responsibilities, offered no escape.

Scraping By

I was seventeen, turning eighteen, and barely holding my life together. I spent my days as a landscaper—the only white kid on a crew where everyone spoke Spanish but me. We rose before dawn and worked until the sun fell, blistering under the Nevada heat, hauling sod, digging trenches, spreading gravel. I couldn't understand their jokes, but I laughed anyway, pretending I belonged.

The money was just enough to pay the bills—rent, utilities, the old truck insurance—but there was never anything left over. In December the season ended, and the work dried up overnight. The crew scattered, promising to call when spring came.

In January I was changing brakes and tires at Pep Boys, the stink of rubber and grease soaked into my hands, living for the moment the clock struck quitting time. I kept telling myself this was temporary, that it wasn't my real life.

But every night I went home to the same dingy house, roommates drunk on the couch, and the same gnawing voice in my head: *Is this all you'll ever be?*

Guard, Not Glory

When I started the paperwork to join the National Guard, it wasn't really patriotism that drove me. It was desperation—the hope that if I could just get far enough from this version of me, maybe I could finally breathe.

The structured discipline of the military presented itself as a refuge, a stark contrast to the bleak prospect of a life mired in poverty and despair. Underlying this was a belief in my own unworthiness, a conviction that I was undeserving of affection, even as I yearned for connection and love with an aching intensity.

The military offered a sense of structure and purpose that seemed like a lifeline. I threw myself into the rigorous routine, seeking to bury the ghosts of my past in physical endurance and mental fortitude. The transformation was almost addictive; I felt myself becoming someone new, someone stronger. The self-doubt remained, but now it was a silent companion, overshadowed by my growing confidence in my abilities. Yet, this newfound power also amplified my destructive impulses, and I found myself walking a tightrope between control and chaos.

Becoming a father at eighteen, then again at twenty, profoundly altered my life's trajectory. Juggling two, sometimes three jobs while my then-wife cared for my increasingly volatile father presented an unrelenting challenge. His unpredictable aggression and desperate attempts to escape to the perceived sanctuary of his youth were emotionally draining. My enlistment in the National Guard as a mechanic, shortly after my firstborn's arrival provided a structured escape. It was a path chosen as much for pragmatism as aspiration.

While I secretly yearned for the elite ranks of Army Rangers or Green Berets, the practical skills I'd honed working on automobiles pointed towards a more attainable career in heavy wheel diesel mechanics. I harbored deep-seated doubts about my capacity to navigate the brutal selection process for special operations.

Finding the Engine

Army basic training's physical training (PT) runs revealed a stark reality. The platoon was divided into four running groups – Alpha, Bravo, Charlie, and Delta – based on ability. Alpha comprised the fleetest; Delta, those struggling to maintain a jog. Initially placing myself in Bravo, I recognized the inherent limitations of a comfortable pace. After two days, I understood stagnation was inevitable. On the third day, I boldly infiltrated the rear of the Alpha group, and through relentless determination, I found myself at the forefront by training's end, a testament to my burgeoning resilience.

Army basic training's rigorous running regimen profoundly shaped my future. It unexpectedly revealed a latent athleticism I never knew existed. This revelation ignited a fierce dedication to mastering the physical fitness test, not just the run. I scavenged a sandbag, meticulously reinforcing it with tape to prevent leakage, transforming it into a powerful tool for self-improvement.

I relentlessly performed weighted push-ups to failure, with the sandbag placed on my neck and shoulders. Crunches followed suit, the sandbag adding significant resistance as it rested heavily on my chest. Post-training, while serving in the Guard, this disciplined approach to fitness persisted. I maintained my rigorous training, consistently achieving a perfect score on every subsequent PT test. This physical transformation mirrored an inner metamorphosis, vanquishing the crippling self-doubt that once held me captive.

Working the Edge

Juggling a demanding forty-hour-a-week job as a power line clearance technician with weekends at the Guard unit was my reality. At first, the sheer verticality terrified me. My first few tall trees triggered waves of vertigo so intense I thought I might black out. One especially tall pine just outside the city swayed in the wind like a ship's mast, the ground spinning far below. I clung to the trunk, forehead pressed against the bark, eyes squeezed shut, willing my body to stay still.

After I learned to climb the safer trees in the city, they transferred me to the dangerous tree crew in the mountains around Tahoe. Our job was to hike the powerline corridors and remove dead trees before they could fall on the transmission lines. The work was brutal, the terrain unforgiving, but something in me responded to it—like I'd finally found a place where my fear could become fuel.

My favorite part came after cutting out a dead top. I would sit back in my saddle, release the tension in my body, and shift my weight back and forth—coaxing the tree into a slow, rolling sway. Soon the whole crown would be rocking back and forth, and I would be flying through the air on the flexing trunk, high above the forest floor, wind chilling my sweat.

It was dangerous. Reckless, even.

But in those moments, suspended between earth and sky, I felt alive in a way nothing else could touch.

That dance with danger felt like freedom—but it was really familiarity. The same nervous system that had grown up bracing for impact now craved the edge of collapse. In hindsight, I can see how that swaying treetop became a rehearsal for what came next. The military promised more of that same electric clarity: risk, control, and the illusion of escape from everything that haunted me on the ground.

Around the same time, I navigated the late-night chaos of a pizza parlor, fulfilling orders and navigating city streets, a stark contrast to my daytime exploits. Even after that ended, I found myself a job working a pre-dawn shift unloading freight at a UPS warehouse before joining the tree crew later in the morning.

Despite this relentless work ethic, my family barely survived. Our cramped one-bedroom apartment—a crib nestled beside our bed, a bunk bed dominating the living space—was a testament to our precarious financial situation. The crushing weight of a foreseeable

future chained to this soul-numbing, repetitive labor fueled a
desperate yearning for escape.

Three years of regular physical training, my accomplishments and
promotions as a diesel mechanic in the National Guard, and my
success as a tree climber had instilled in me a confidence that I had
never known before.

This emboldened me to pursue active duty in the military – a
decision driven by the promise of enhanced financial security, stable
housing, and comprehensive healthcare for my family. Beyond
material benefits, the prospect of confronting a more demanding
military challenge ignited a fierce internal drive.

Ranger Dreams, Recon Road

A burning need consumed me—to shatter the limiting, self-fulfilling
prophecy my mother had cast upon me: the feeling that I would
never do anything of consequence. My initial foray into this
transition involved an Army recruiter, my goal being the elite Army
Ranger program. However, his negligence and lack of responsiveness
left me deeply frustrated. I reclaimed my application materials and,
fueled by determination, walked into a Marine Corps recruiting
office.

By then, I was in the best shape of my life—running twenty to thirty
miles a week, strength training every other day, sparring at a boxing
gym, swimming laps a few nights a week. My body was sharp and
ready. My mind was another story. I was terrified of the Marines. I'd
read books and heard stories about their brutal training and
unrelenting discipline, and part of me doubted I could measure up.

The recruiter who greeted me looked like the embodiment of
everything I feared and wanted—jacked, posture like steel, his tan
short-sleeved shirt crisp, the blood-red stripes on his sharply creased
blue trousers like slashes of war paint.

Upon presenting my documents, he responded concisely, "This is all I require. What's your occupational preference?" His tone was all efficiency, no sales pitch—like he was interviewing me for a place in something sacred.

My gaze locked onto a poster on the wall: Recon Marines, navigating dense jungles and slipping through the ocean's depths. "That," I said, pointing. "That's what I want."

A confident grin spread across his face. "You can't directly enlist in Recon," he explained. "Infantry is the entry point—you'll earn your place with them if you can pass their tests. Can you swim?"

"Yeah," I said, leaning forward in the chair. "I can swim. Sign me up."

The decision to pursue a path as a Marine was a pivotal moment, marking a turning point in my life. The recruiter's words, "You can't directly enlist in Recon," were a challenge, and I was determined to prove myself once more. I embraced the opportunity to start as infantry, knowing that my goal of joining the special unit was within reach if I could pass their tests.

And so, I found myself facing a new set of trials, both physical and mental, as I prepared for the demands of Marine life. The rigorous training and structured discipline of the Marines became my new obsession, a means to continue the transformation I had begun in the National Guard. I pushed myself to the limits, determined to earn my place among the elite.

Armor That Fits

In those early days of the Marine Corps, I believed I had finally outrun the chaos. The structure, the standards, the discipline—it all felt like proof that I wasn't broken after all. For the first time in my life, I felt chosen, valuable, even powerful. The pain I had carried from childhood—the fear, the rage, the constant readiness for betrayal—seemed like a gift now, a cruel but effective preparation.

I told myself that my experiences had forged me into something stronger. I wore that belief like armor, convincing myself that the past no longer mattered, that I had mastered it. But the truth was, I was still trapped in it.

I couldn't yet see the ways I had bonded to my abusers, the way I still needed pain to feel purpose, control to feel safe, and punishment to feel loved. I was deep in denial, convinced I had overcome what I had only buried deeper.

From instability and abuse to obsession and overwork, my path reveals a desperate hunger to become someone else—someone worthy of love and belonging. I didn't know who I was—but I knew who I didn't want to be.

I wasn't trying to grow; I was trying to escape. Each job, each push-up, each climb into the treetops wasn't just about survival—it was about constructing a self from scratch, a self that might finally be worthy of love and respect. But no matter how much I achieved, I carried the same core belief: that I had to earn my right to exist.

The identity I crafted—first as a diesel mechanic, then as a budding warrior—was both armor and disguise. I wore confidence on the outside, but inside, I was still the boy my mother had belittled, the one I was terrified of still being. I trusted systems more than people. I believed in punishment more than praise.

My capacity for connection had been hollowed out by betrayal, so I kept others at arm's length, even those I loved. That's why it felt easier—almost freeing—to leave my young family behind. The ache I felt for them was real, but it was also familiar, and I had grown comfortable in my solitude.

Every chance I got to take leave, I did. I'd drive the eight hours home, push through the night, and stay until the last possible moment before turning back, barely enough time to make formation. It was like living two separate lives—and being two separate people.

I remember standing at the door, my duffel slung over my shoulder, the boys clinging to my legs. My oldest was old enough to understand I was leaving again; his face was wet with tears. My youngest just laughed and wrapped his little arms tighter around my legs, thinking it was a game. I felt nothing.

And I hated that I felt nothing.

I didn't have words for any of this back then. All I knew was that I felt built differently—like I was made for chaos, like calm was dangerous and closeness was a risk I couldn't afford. Years later, desperate to understand why I could feel safe in a warzone but not at home, I began studying trauma. What I discovered helped me see that none of this was random—there was a map to the way my life had taken shape.

That was the cost of the armor: the same numbness that kept me safe on the battlefield kept me distant from the people I loved most.

I told myself this was the price of becoming someone new—that love could wait until I was finally worthy of it.

In the Marine Corps, I believed I had finally found the version of myself that could not be hurt, that could not be questioned. But in truth, I had only found a place where my wounds could function like strengths. The very traits that helped me survive childhood— hypervigilance, emotional distance, relentless drive—now earned me accolades. The military didn't heal me; it made me believe I didn't need healing. And that belief, more than anything else, would come to haunt me in the years that followed.

When I joined the Marines, it wasn't just about serving my country—it was about finding a self. I needed an identity built on strength, purpose, and control, one that could overwrite the shame and helplessness I'd grown up with. The Corps gave me structure and meaning, a brotherhood where power was currency and suffering had value. I felt like I belonged. I told myself I was finally becoming who I was meant to be.

But in truth, I was still running. The emotional distance I kept from my wife and sons wasn't an accident—it was armor. I told myself they would be better off with a name on a check than a presence in their lives. And deep down, I was relieved to leave. Adventure, danger, and discipline were easier than intimacy. The Marine Corps didn't just give me a mission—it gave me permission to keep my heart walled off. I wasn't just escaping poverty. I was escaping the parts of myself I didn't yet know how to face.

It would take me years to understand why I felt that way. Back then, I thought I was simply wired differently. Only much later—after war, after collapse, after therapy—would I begin to learn the language of trauma, and how it had shaped my body, my brain, and my very sense of self. The science gave me names for what I had lived, and it revealed that none of it was random.

The way I moved through the world, the way I trusted systems more than people, the way I could feel calm in a warzone but not at home—it all had a story behind it.

I couldn't see it at the time. Back then, I thought I was just built for chaos—that something in me was naturally suited to danger, to conflict, to war, like something in me only came alive when everything was on fire. Only later would I learn that what I called "strength" was really adaptation—that my body and brain had been shaped by the constant stress of my childhood. The instincts that made me thrive in combat had been forged long before I ever held a rifle.

ACE Patterns

Childhood trauma doesn't just hurt—it builds. It builds patterns in the brain, defense systems in the body, and belief systems in the psyche. When we grow up in homes shaped by violence, abandonment, chaos, or neglect, we don't leave those experiences behind when we become adults. We carry them in our nervous systems, our hormones, our muscle memory, and our emotional defaults.

The trauma becomes architecture—shaping not only how we feel but who we become. For many, that architecture points us toward high-stress, high-control, or violent professions. The battlefield outside eventually mirrors the one that formed us inside.

This idea is no longer just poetic. It's now well documented in neuroscience, psychology, and epidemiology. The **Adverse Childhood Experiences (ACE) Study**, conducted by Felitti et al. (1998), found that the more traumatic experiences a child endures—such as physical abuse, sexual abuse, emotional neglect, or household dysfunction—the greater their risk for a staggering range of health problems in adulthood: depression, substance abuse, heart disease, autoimmune disorders, cancer, and premature death. But the ACE study also reveals another, less discussed outcome: many people who score high on ACEs also seek out extreme environments in adulthood—not despite their trauma, but because of it.

But ACEs aren't just about statistics. They don't stay sealed in the past. They show up again, in ways you don't expect, unless the cycle is broken.

I didn't fully understand that until years later, when I watched the same violence I had endured as a boy echo forward into another generation.

I was at a holiday gathering. I'd slipped away from the noise and found a bench in the dining room, playing chess on my phone. My mother was the only other person in the room. One of the toddlers — three, maybe four years old — came running in, bare as the day he was born, climbing up on the table and laughing.

And then I saw it.

Her arm shot out, fingers clamped on his penis.
Her voice, cold and sharp: *"You go put some clothes on or I'll cut this off."*

He screamed. I moved without thinking, lifting him off the table and setting him on the ground. His legs pumping in the air before they touched the floor. He bolted. I watched him go and then turned to face her. She just looked at me with that familiar sneer — the same expression she wore when I defied her as a boy.

Later, in therapy, I told the story. Halfway through, my therapist stopped me gently. *"Anthony, I'm a mandated reporter. I have to contact CPS."*

At first, I didn't understand. Then I remember laughing — not because it was funny, but because for the first time in my life, someone outside the family saw her clearly.

That moment marked something I hadn't recognized until then: silence was no longer loyalty. It was complicity.

Researchers call this *intergenerational trauma*: the way unresolved abuse is passed down not through stories, but through nervous systems, through behaviors and silences that become family law. (Yehuda & Lehrner, 2018) The ACE study doesn't just measure what happens to children. It shows what happens when no one intervenes: the cycle repeats.

Breaking that silence to protect a child was the first time I acted against my wiring. For decades, I had mistaken secrecy for love and suffering for loyalty. Speaking up cracked the armor. And through the crack, I could finally see the truth: what we bury doesn't disappear. It waits, it festers, and then it resurfaces in the next set of small hands and wide eyes — unless somebody decides the cycle ends here.

To understand how early trauma predisposes people toward high-stress professions or even violence, we have to start with the brain. When a child is raised in an environment where safety is uncertain, their **amygdala**—the brain's fear and threat-detection center—becomes hyperactive. Meanwhile, the **prefrontal cortex**, which governs logic, planning, and impulse control, lags behind. The **hippocampus**, which helps contextualize memory and separate past from present, can also shrink in volume when exposed to chronic stress (Teicher et al., 2003).

In practical terms, this means the brain of a traumatized child becomes wired not for connection, but for defense. Hypervigilance becomes the default mode. Emotional outbursts become harder to regulate. And because trauma often happens in relationships, the nervous system begins to treat closeness itself as a threat.

Dr. **Bessel van der Kolk**, in *The Body Keeps the Score* (2014), writes that trauma doesn't just affect what we remember—it changes how we physically experience the world. Traumatized individuals often have a "low threshold for alarm," reacting to perceived threats with a fight-or-flight response, even when no real danger is present. This neurobiological pattern can be deeply maladaptive in civilian life— but in combat zones, emergency response units, or violent subcultures, it becomes an asset. The same traits that make it hard to sit in a classroom or trust a romantic partner make someone exceptionally valuable in a fight.

It's not a coincidence that so many people in the military, law enforcement, firefighting, or combat sports have high ACE scores. According to a 2015 study by Pacella et al., first responders had significantly higher ACE scores than the general population. Veterans, especially those who enlist at a young age, often report a background of early adversity, including poverty, unstable homes, or abuse. A 2018 study published in *Military Medicine* found that ACE scores were positively correlated with risk-taking behavior and combat exposure.

Why is this?

Part of the reason is practical: for many traumatized youths, the military is one of the only accessible paths out of poverty, addiction, or chaotic environments. But on a deeper level, high-stress institutions can feel oddly familiar. The unpredictability, the need for control, the high stakes, the black-and-white moral codes—they echo the internal world of a traumatized child.

Shadow at the Wheel

Gabor Maté, in *In the Realm of Hungry Ghosts* (2010), explains that many people are "addicted" to danger, adrenaline, or overwork because it distracts from unresolved pain. He writes: "Trauma is not what happens to you. Trauma is what happens inside you as a result of what happens to you." A child who feels powerless may grow into an adult who compulsively seeks power—especially the kind of power that comes with weapons, orders, uniforms, and precision. Not because it heals them—but because it helps them function.

In some cases, people who grew up in violent or chaotic homes become "adrenaline junkies," not for thrill-seeking alone, but because being calm feels unsafe. As Dr. Maté notes, "If you grew up in chaos, calm feels unfamiliar—and therefore dangerous." High-stress environments become a kind of psychological homeostasis. Danger is the devil you know.

Carl Jung offered a deeper spiritual and psychological insight into how trauma shapes identity. He believed that everyone possesses a "shadow"—the unconscious, hidden part of the psyche that contains both our wounds and our potential. Left unexamined, the shadow governs us without our knowing. "Until you make the unconscious conscious," Jung wrote, "it will direct your life and you will call it fate" (Jung, 1953).

For those with traumatic childhoods, the shadow is often filled with shame, fear, and anger. If those energies are not integrated or healed, they will find expression in compulsive behaviors, self-sabotage, or externalized violence. This is one reason why many trauma survivors feel "driven"—to overachieve, to prove themselves, or to punish themselves. The military offers a crucible where this drive can be channeled—and even rewarded.

But without healing, this alignment becomes a trap. We begin to confuse our trauma adaptations for personality traits. Hypervigilance becomes "discipline." Numbness becomes "stoicism." Isolation becomes "self-reliance." The wounded child within us never stops trying to earn love—often through suffering, performance, or sacrifice.

While psychology and neuroscience reveal how trauma reshapes the brain, it also imprints itself into the body. Peter Levine, founder of Somatic Experiencing, emphasizes that trauma is "stored in the body" as incomplete fight-or-flight responses (Levine, 1997/2010). Survivors often live with chronic tension, digestive issues, autoimmune conditions, or unexplained pain—physical echoes of the stress their bodies never got to release. Long after the danger has passed, the nervous system remains caught in a loop of unfinished survival, trying even decades later to resolve what could not be escaped in childhood.

And still—we praise the "grit." We reward the discipline, the toughness, the loyalty. We put uniforms and medals over the places that ache the most and call it transformation.

Understanding trauma isn't about assigning blame or stripping away agency. It's about recognizing that the strategies we developed to survive childhood—vigilance, withdrawal, people-pleasing, aggression—were brilliant adaptations. But they are not the same thing as healing. Without awareness, these strategies direct our choices, shape our identity, and drive us toward environments that reinforce our wounds.

To heal is not to discard our past. It's to finally hold it with compassion. It's to recognize that survival was never the goal—only the starting point.

Homer knew what many of us learn only through brutal experience: that suffering is not a place we leave behind, it is contained in our shadow everywhere we go. The illusion of escape, seductive as it may be, ultimately dissolves, leaving us face-to-face with the truth we most fear: that our wounds remain with us until they are faced, understood, and integrated.

My own escape route took the form of military life—a world of clear expectations, rigid structures, and unequivocal rules. The chaos of childhood, the constant threat of violence and abandonment, left me desperate for stability. The Marines promised exactly that: a chance to remake myself in a disciplined, structured environment. I embraced their physical challenges, their emotional distance, their focus on performance over feeling. For a while, it seemed as though I had found the solution to my suffering. I was stronger, tougher, more resilient—or so I thought.

Homer's wisdom lies not merely in his recognition of suffering's inevitability but in his implicit understanding that attempts at escape often deepen the very pain we seek to avoid. Achilles retreats into rage; Odysseus wanders aimlessly for years; each hero attempts escape through strength, cunning, or defiance—and each fails.

I too, attempted escape through relentless work, through the pain of physical endurance, and through the camaraderie of men who shared similar wounds. Yet each attempt left me further from peace, further from connection, further from genuine healing.

Becoming a father at such a young age had offered me a different path, a chance at intimacy, vulnerability, and connection. But I was not yet capable of embracing it. Fatherhood required emotional availability—precisely the thing my trauma had stripped from me. The fear of repeating my parents' failures was overwhelming. The structured world of the military felt safer, clearer, easier than the messiness of love and family.

As Jung observed, until we bring our shadows into consciousness, we will live under their control, mistaking their influence for fate. My enlistment in the Marines, my obsession with physical strength, my pride in endurance—all seemed like purposeful choices. Yet beneath each decision was a hidden compulsion, an unconscious drive to escape suffering by burying myself in environments that mirrored my traumatic past.

The brutality of boot camp, the fierce demands of infantry training, the harsh judgment of military discipline—they all felt familiar. I was comfortable in a world defined by suffering because it mirrored the emotional landscape of my childhood.

Only when I began to consciously unpack the layers of trauma did I realize how deeply I had internalized my wounds. My resilience, discipline, and hypervigilance—traits the Marines valued—were all born from trauma. They were survival strategies, not healing strategies. The armor I wore had protected me but also trapped me, sealing in my wounds along with my strengths.

The neuroscience is clear: trauma reshapes the brain, wiring it not for love and intimacy, but for threat and defense. Early experiences of fear, abandonment, or abuse engrave patterns into our neural architecture that persist long after the threat itself is gone. The hyperactive amygdala, the impaired hippocampus, the weakened prefrontal cortex—these are the unseen scars of childhood trauma. Military life didn't heal these wounds; it merely put them to use, reinforcing patterns that made civilian life all the more challenging to navigate.

I didn't know any of this then. At eighteen, I couldn't have told you what an amygdala was or how trauma rewires the brain. I just knew that structure felt safer than chaos, that discipline felt cleaner than despair.

The science came later—years later—when I was trying to understand why my life had taken the shape it had. Only in hindsight could I see how the traits that made me thrive in the military were all forged in the furnace of my childhood.

Back then, I wasn't seeking healing. I was seeking escape. The Corps wasn't a solution; it was an exoskeleton I could crawl into, a place where my wounds could look like strengths.

For the first time in my life, I wasn't just surviving chaos.
I was entering a world that manufactured it on purpose—and demanded I become one with it.

Yellow Footprints

The first day of Marine Corps boot camp feels like it will never end. You step off the bus onto the yellow footprints in the early evening—and they keep you awake all night. Gear issue, haircuts, paperwork, screaming. The next day blurs into more: clothing issue, admin lines, the relentless bark of orders. By the time we finally staggered into our squad bay with our gear, it had been over twenty-four hours since sleep.

That's when they marched us to the showers.

The drill instructors, screaming as always, packed us shoulder to shoulder against the wall of the showers, skin slick and pale under the buzzing lights. We tried to maintain our distance. "Nut to butt," they barked, pushing us closer and then—unbelievably—"Sit."
We couldn't actually sit. We had to collapse backward into the man behind us and accept the weight of the man in front.

Any trace of individuality was gone. We were bodies now. Interchangeable. Erased.

What should have been dehumanizing felt strangely familiar to me. The screaming, the humiliation, the volatility—it mirrored the world I'd been raised in. The difference was that this chaos had rules. It wasn't personal. It was predictable.

After that, the blur began: close-order drill, punishing workouts, endless "corrective training." Because I was taller than everyone, any mistake I made during close order drill stood out, and I got singled out constantly for extra thrashings.

I refused to break.

By the time we reached the field phase and the long final hike they call the Crucible, I had found my stride. Where others were shrinking, I was growing. Literally.

Most recruits lose weight in boot camp. I gained nearly forty pounds. One of the underweight recruits gave me his extra "double rations" chit, and I used it like a weapon. I slammed milk, yogurt, fruit, and as much hot chow as I could get down my throat in the short time we were allowed to eat. The drill instructors took notice and tried to make me puke it out afterward with endless punishing workouts.

I never puked.
I never gave them the satisfaction.

Boot camp didn't break me. It fed the part of me that already knew how to survive in chaos. But surviving is not the same as healing— and Homer seemed to understand that.

Honor the Child

Homer's words also carry an implicit promise: if no escape truly works, perhaps the solution lies not in running but in turning towards our suffering. Healing begins not by denying pain, but by acknowledging it. The wounds we carry from childhood do not have to remain hidden beneath uniforms, achievements, or physical endurance; they can be acknowledged, confronted, and ultimately integrated into a deeper understanding of ourselves.

This recognition doesn't erase our pain, but it transforms our relationship to it. Understanding trauma as a foundational force in our lives offers the chance to reclaim agency. It allows us to stop mistaking compulsive behaviors for personality traits and begin the slower, harder work of genuine self-knowledge and self-compassion.

My journey taught me that true strength lies not in outrunning our shadows, but in facing them directly. I understand now what Homer implied centuries ago: that our attempts at escape only delay our healing. Suffering can never be outrun—but it can be understood, integrated, and ultimately transformed.

Today, I strive not to erase my wounds but to accept them. I honor the child I once was—not for his ability to survive trauma, but for his humanity, his vulnerability, and his enduring desire for love. The gods may have given us many ways to escape suffering, none of which truly work. But they also gave us the capacity for reflection, awareness, and healing. These are the tools that can finally transform suffering—not into strength alone, but into wisdom, compassion, and genuine connection.

Homer's wisdom endures because it speaks directly to the heart of our humanity. Suffering, he reminds us, is inevitable. Escape is impossible. But healing—real, honest healing—is always within reach.

What Endures

Looking back, I can see that what I mistook for strength was simply adaptation. Boot camp didn't forge a new man; it refined the one my childhood had already shaped. The discipline, the structure, the controlled chaos—all of it gave my wounds a place to function, not a chance to heal. I had built my identity on endurance, but endurance alone can't teach you how to be whole.

That would come much later, after the battles and the accolades, after the armor began to crack. What I carried into the Marines wasn't just drive or determination—it was a wounded boy's desperate hope that becoming unbreakable would make him worthy of love. I see now that true strength is not about becoming unbreakable, but about becoming real—and real things can break. They can also heal.

I thought I had left the chaos behind, but what I didn't yet understand was that I had only carried it deeper inside, where it would burn slow and quiet until the war gave it oxygen.

The military gave me a way forward, but really it was the same path I had always been walking. My body had been wired for battle long before I signed a contract. The abuse, the exile, the constant readiness — all of it had trained me to function in chaos. Boot camp didn't rewire me; it confirmed me.

What I didn't understand then was that there is more than one kind of trauma. The wounds from childhood didn't vanish when I put on a uniform — they fused with the new wounds war would deliver. That's what made them so powerful, and so hard to name.

In combat, trauma doesn't always explode in a single moment. Sometimes it lingers, embedding itself in the body like shrapnel you can't see. The military acronym for it: PTSD. But what I lived was bigger, stranger, and more insidious than what could be summed up in those letters.

War doesn't just mark a single day — it burns itself into the rhythm of your life, a fire that refuses to go out.

Part II: Scraping Off the Label
Rejecting PTSD and Naming the Real Wounds of War

"That my fury could drive me to carve and eat you raw for the wrongs you have done me. No ransom will save you from the dogs."

— Homer, *The Iliad*, Book XXII, public domain translation (adapted)

Chapter 3: The Fire That Won't Go Out
Understanding Sustained Stress Injuries Beyond the PTSD Model

"Of all creatures that breathe and move upon the earth, nothing is bred that is weaker than man. For he thinks that he shall never suffer evil in time to come, so long as the gods grant him prosperity and his knees are nimble. But when again the blessed gods bring sorrow upon him, this too he bears in his heart with steadfastness, enduring it by the necessity of fate."

— Homer, *The Odyssey*, Book XVII, trans. A.T. Murray, 1919 (public domain)

It's An Injury

The first time I felt it, I didn't call it trauma. I called it being alive. Combat sharpened me the way childhood had prepared me to be sharpened — a body humming with adrenaline, a mind split between numbness and hypervigilance, a soul burning quietly underneath it all. Long after the firefights ended, the fire stayed lit. Not a blaze you can stamp out, but a low flame that eats through the nights, through marriages, through every quiet moment when the world expects you to be at peace.

My understanding of sustained stress injuries is from my own experiences and conversations with fellow combat veterans. As a security contractor I worked on a job where the minimum qualification was five years of special operations experience, so I got to work with all types. If you are curious about the differences between military special operations units, I can assure you that they are minimal and mainly attributable to the culture of the unit and their budget. All of them have some really good men, some not so good men, and everything in between.

The time that I spent among them, working the streets of Afghanistan, was the most alive that I have ever felt.

I chose the term sustained stress injury as part of my efforts to better understand and be able to explain the different parts of my experiences in combat and their unique effects. I needed language that matched how this really felt in a body, not just a diagnosis on paper. I posit that sustained stress injuries are the most prevalent form of trauma among combat veterans, arising from chronic exposure to exceptionally high stress levels.

This prolonged exposure forces profound physiological adaptations within the brain to manage the surge of stress hormones. **(Mason et al., 2001; van der Kolk, 2014)** I believe this phenomenon extends beyond the military, affecting law enforcement personnel, first responders, and even prisoners. Anyone confined to perpetually stressful environments will ultimately adapt. The body and mind acclimate to this hyper-stress, establishing a new baseline.

Upon returning to a less demanding civilian life, the absence of this intense stimulation creates profound difficulties in readjustment. Individuals subconsciously seek to replicate that adrenaline surge, to get that familiar high again. Multiple deployments exacerbate this effect, profoundly altering their perception of "normal" life.

Many of my colleagues thrived under intense operational pressure, finding inactivity and boredom intolerable. A relentless workload facilitates a positive mental state; idleness, however, fosters a breeding ground for homesickness and the agonizing weight of severed familial and social bonds.

Kabul Tempo

This was especially true of me; I can't sit still. My supervisor
intercepted me in the hotel hallway during my final deployment to
Kabul as a contractor. He declared, with genuine admiration, that if
he possessed the authority to bestow an accolade, I would be its
recipient. Intrigued, I inquired about the nature of this hypothetical
commendation. He revealed that I had completed an astounding 144
assignments within a mere 114 days—a feat that left him utterly
bewildered.

I lived like a man on fire.

While most contractors paced themselves—four or five runs a week,
time to hit the gym, maybe call home—I was out the gate twice a
day, sometimes more, snatching every mission that popped up on the
board before anyone else could claim it. The city became my
obsession. Kabul's streets wound through me like veins, pumping
adrenaline instead of blood.

I knew every route—the smooth blacktop arteries lined with blast
walls, the dusty backroads where kids played soccer barefoot, the
claustrophobic alleys that could turn from quiet to kill-zone in a
blink. I memorized choke points, traffic patterns, the rhythm of the
city's breathing. I could feel when something was off, when the air
got tight, when the hairs rose on the back of my neck.

Sleep became optional. Meals were fuel stops. My world shrank to
steel doors slamming, engines rumbling, radios hissing, and the ever-
present Glock 17 on my hip. I didn't want breaks. Breaks meant
thinking. Thinking meant feeling. So, I stayed in motion.

Each run was its own small war—a gauntlet of checkpoints, crowded
intersections, sudden dead-ends that forced split-second decisions.
My hands were always steady on the wheel, but inside I was burning.
The adrenaline sharpened everything: the colors, the edges, the
sound of my own breath. It felt like clarity. It felt like power.

But really, it was survival. If I stopped moving, the weight of everything I hadn't faced would catch up to me. So, I didn't stop. Not for anything.

What felt like drive was really desperation—a refusal to be still long enough for the buried things to surface. That compulsion to keep moving wasn't unique to me; it's baked into the culture of high-stress military environments. The longer we stayed in that rhythm, the more it rewired us, until exhaustion became normal and rest felt dangerous.

In the military's special operations units, that compulsion is almost ritualized—constant movement, punishing operational tempo, and fractured sleep cycles. We often went days without real rest, relying on stimulants to keep going. My choice was coffee, but many guys turned to over-the-counter amphetamines just to stay upright.

Sleep-Deprived Visions

The most vivid hallucinations I experienced came from that exhaustion.
One night we were on patrol in Fallujah, clearing structures for Marine occupation on the city's edge. It was night, and we'd been awake for well over twenty-four hours—maybe longer. We snatched sleep when we could, dozing upright in the heat of the day until someone nudged us or flicked our helmets to wake us up. My uniform was soaked through with sweat from jumping walls, climbing stairs, and scaling ladders, while wearing 60 pounds of armor, ammo, and water.

When we patrolled out of the urban sprawl into irrigated farmland, we stopped for a quick break. There were five other men in my team, and we were linking up with the rest of the platoon nearby. I had this habit of counting my team during halts at night, just to make sure everyone was still there.

I scanned them in the green-and-black glow of my night vision as they knelt in a defensive circle, each man facing outboard, sipping water, eyes locked on their sectors. I counted them. One, two, three… all the way to sixteen.

But I only had five.

Even as I realized it couldn't be real, I could still see them—shapes where there were no men, figures overlapping and shifting like smoke. I stood and walked toward one of them, convinced that if I just reached out I could make sense of what I was seeing.

A whisper cut through my headset: "What are you doing?"

I lifted my NVGs. The false figures evaporated. I was pawing at empty air, yards away from the real team, who were all watching me.

I walked back and dropped to a knee in the center of their circle. "I need some sleep," I said quietly. "Let's move."

On another night during that same deployment, the roles were reversed. I was jolted awake by my platoon sergeant in the early morning hours. We were on a 50% rest plan—half of us sleeping while the other half stood watch. At no point should every Marine be asleep; someone is always responsible for security.

He whispered urgently, shaking me, telling me he needed me to call in a fire mission from the nearby mortar team. As soon as I saw his eyes, wide and glassy behind a large set of humming thermal binoculars, I knew he was hallucinating. He insisted he could see a company-sized element of enemy fighters moving toward our position.

I asked to confirm the target and he handed me the thermals. Through the glowing haze, I saw only a scattered herd of sheep grazing in the dark. We argued in hushed tones, his voice tight with certainty, mine with disbelief. Finally, I flatly refused to get on the radio.

Had it been anyone else he woke, they might have leveled that field—and some poor farmer's flock with it. Maybe that's why he chose me.

Adaptation, Not Event

I knew what had happened, even then. It wasn't madness—it was exhaustion. My brain was starting to slip, rewriting reality just to keep me moving. That was the cost of living on the edge for too long: the boundary between perception and hallucination thinned until even your senses stopped trusting you.

We were raised in a culture that glorified the blaze but never taught us how to rest, and so we mistook the slow burn of our undoing for purpose.

That same culture drew clear lines between war and home, but for those of us who lived inside the blaze, the boundary was never so clean. The shift from the adrenaline-fueled world of combat to the muted rhythms of civilian life is stark—and it's one many veterans struggle to navigate. The high-stress environment of combat becomes a familiar, addictive state of being (Maté, 2010). It's a fire that rages within, ignited by the relentless pressure and intensity of those experiences. This fire becomes their constant companion, shaping their perceptions and driving their actions.

What I thought was just my own restless fire was not mine alone. It was the shape of a nervous system forged in unending tension, the same haunted rhythm I would later see flickering behind the eyes of so many others who came home. What felt like drive was really the echo of survival—what I would come to call a sustained stress injury.

Under Rocket Fire

My personal experience with sustained stress has illuminated the plight of many fellow veterans outside direct combat roles. Consider, for instance, the aircraft mechanic stationed on a forward operating base. Though never leaving the relative safety of the base perimeter, they endure the relentless psychological onslaught of regular mortar and rocket attacks. The sheer helplessness, the knowledge that deadly ordnance might fall at any moment, coupled with witnessing the devastation inflicted on colleagues, creates profound and enduring stress. This constant, inescapable threat generates an intensity of suffering often overlooked.

In 2004, I was in Fallujah, Iraq. The military camp, just a short drive from the city, received mortar and rocket fire almost daily. On the day I arrived, a mortar hit one of the portable toilets—luckily no one was inside. Not long after, a rocket flew through a two-foot window and killed a major at his desk. That became the backdrop to daily life: the unspoken knowledge that death could drop from the sky at any moment.

We acted cool, but it was all performance. Every walk across the camp was a quiet calculation of the nearest cover. At the first wail of the siren—or worse, the sudden banshee scream of incoming rockets—we'd sprint for whatever protection was closest. Once, I remember bursting from a latrine, pants half-down, diving between two close buildings as explosions shook the ground. When the volley finally stopped, a giddy rush would flood through us, and we'd lean on our dark humor to lift the mood, laughing harder than the moment deserved.

You never really relaxed after that. Even in the chow hall, in the gym, brushing your teeth—some part of you stayed coiled. You were never just *there*. You were always halfway to cover, halfway to gone. That's what living under sustained threat does: it rewires you. It teaches your body that safety is a lie.

Patrol Rhythm

After the first two months of continuous combat operations in the city of Fallujah, we moved into the camp outside the city. We settled into a routine of 24 hours on patrol followed by 24 hours off patrol for the next five months. When we were on patrol, we conducted a variety of tasks ranging from reconnaissance to direct action raids of the villages around the city. While we feared the random rockets and mortars on base, outside of it, we were always watchful for roadside IEDs and enemy ambushes.

Our deployment in Fallujah began with a brutal ambush only a few weeks after our arrival. The ensuing chaos – the dead and wounded – triggered a reshuffling of personnel. My friend, lacerated by shrapnel, was reassigned to a rear-echelon post, his recovery confined to the relative safety of the base. One morning, exhausted after a grueling 24-hour patrol, I had put all my gear away and was preparing for a much-needed rest. Suddenly, he erupted into the space, a wild, shrieking figure lunging at me. His intent, he later claimed, was to be funny.

Instead, terror seized me. Blind fury consumed me; I reacted violently, seizing his uniform collar and hurling him across the room. His screams were lost in my rage, a maelstrom that only subsided after an agonizing 30 seconds. Tears welled, blurring my vision. I apologized, and we hugged it out. That was my reality: a veneer of stoicism masking a volatile core, perpetually teetering on the brink of madness.

Baseline of Burn

Returning from deployment, I collapsed into my barracks room, slumbering for a week, punctuated only by hurried trips to the mess hall. My nerves were frayed, raw. The vibrant, bustling SoCal social scene felt utterly alien, a jarring contrast to the past seven months. Every waking moment had been consumed by a hypervigilance, a relentless scanning for threats. Relaxation was impossible; I understood that recovery would demand considerable time and profound rest.

Emerging from my confinement, the familiar world felt profoundly estranged, a landscape inhabited by a stranger's life. Everywhere, the garish yellow ribbons and "Support the Troops" banners assaulted my senses. While ostensibly well-meaning, this public display struck me as a grotesque façade, a cosmetic fix applied to a dwelling, rife with unspeakable horrors.

Their cheerful patriotism was a willful blindness, a refusal to acknowledge the monstrous realities lurking within—realities they preferred to conceal beneath a veneer of normalcy, a desperate attempt to integrate a haunted house into the pristine suburban landscape, ignoring the tormented souls within.

Toward the culmination of our Fallujah deployment, a call went out: volunteers needed for the Marine Expeditionary Unit (MEU) platoon. A MEU—a constantly deployed, globally-responsive force—required augmentation. The entire battalion's commitment to Fallujah meant that any selected Marine would face immediate, relentless duty.

Deployment's end wouldn't bring respite; instead, a grueling six-month training regimen would commence, launching them directly into the MEU's next operation. My company, brimming with battle-hardened veterans—adrenaline-fueled warriors who'd fought at the front of the 2003 invasion and returned for the 2004 Fallujah fight—responded instantly. The platoon filled with eager volunteers in a heartbeat. I was among them.

Sustained stress had become my baseline; the truth was, I harbored a profound aversion to returning to normalcy. A life spent in the crucible of conflict held a strange appeal; I yearned for its perpetual intensity. The prospect of a shortened lifespan, even a violent end on foreign soil mirroring my fallen comrades' fates, seemed preferable to the soul-crushing banality of civilian existence, a life of drudgery toiling under the yoke of societal expectations.

PTSD's Limits

While Post-Traumatic Stress Disorder (PTSD) has become the dominant framework for understanding combat-related psychological injuries, it fails to fully capture the reality of many veterans' lived experiences. For those who served in high-tempo, multi-deployment environments, trauma is not always rooted in a single horrific event. Instead, it accumulates gradually, through prolonged exposure to extreme stress. This is what many veterans, including myself, understand as a sustained stress injury—a chronic, adaptive injury caused not by one explosion, but by years spent in a mental and physiological state of constant readiness.

PTSD was originally conceptualized around acute trauma: a car crash, a rape, a bombing. But sustained stress is different. It builds slowly and invisibly, over weeks, months, and years. There may be no single triggering event. Rather, it's the cumulative effect of hypervigilance, operational pressure, emotional suppression, and sleep deprivation that rewires the brain and body over time.

Gabor Maté (2010) argues that trauma should not be defined by the event itself, but by the internal response to it. From this lens, sustained exposure to combat zones—where danger is omnipresent, relationships are transitory, and adrenaline is constant—produces an internal reality that is indistinguishable from trauma. "Stress is not the enemy," Maté writes. "It's unrelieved stress. The chronic repetition of stress, with no relief and no time to heal, changes us biologically."

Hyperarousal Normal

Combat does not just create momentary stress; it teaches the body to normalize it. Bessel van der Kolk (2014) explains that trauma imprints itself somatically, particularly in the autonomic nervous system. For veterans, the sympathetic nervous system—responsible for fight or flight—can become dominant. Over time, the body forgets how to relax.

This is reinforced by the military lifestyle itself: rotating shifts, long deployments, mission unpredictability, and constant scanning for threats. In neuroscience, this is described as allostatic load—the cumulative wear and tear on the body from chronic stress. The stress-response system, particularly the hypothalamic-pituitary-adrenal (HPA) axis, begins to misfire. The result is a brain that is "always on"—wired for danger, regardless of the environment. Studies show that prolonged stress causes:

• Elevated cortisol and norepinephrine levels (Mason et al., 2001)
• Structural changes in the hippocampus (memory) and amygdala (threat detection)
• Increased risk of cardiovascular disease, immune dysregulation, and gastrointestinal disorders (McEwen, 2006)

Even after returning home, many veterans continue to live in a physiological state that mirrors combat readiness. This leads to emotional numbness, insomnia, explosive anger, and an inability to tolerate ordinary civilian life.

The Addiction to Intensity

Another underexplored facet of sustained stress injuries is the adrenaline addiction that often forms in response. Combat offers a uniquely heightened state of being—clear purpose, physical danger, total focus. For some, it is the first time they've ever felt truly alive.

Maté notes that addiction is not about the substance or behavior itself, but the pain it masks and the temporary relief it provides. In this light, adrenaline becomes a drug. When it is removed—when the deployments end, the missions stop, and the routine disappears—the withdrawal begins. Many veterans feel depressed, aimless, or angry. They chase new risks (reckless driving, extreme sports, high-stakes jobs), not to be dangerous, but to feel like themselves again.

This phenomenon is echoed in military research. A study published in *Military Medicine* (Brenner et al., 2015) found that service members with high deployment tempo showed increased difficulty adjusting to garrison or civilian life, and a strong correlation between tempo and maladaptive coping behaviors.

The Warrior Archetype and the Identity Crisis

Carl Jung's concept of the archetype offers a psychological frame for understanding why sustained stress becomes addictive. The "warrior" archetype is deeply embedded in the collective unconscious—representing strength, discipline, sacrifice, and loyalty. In combat, the warrior archetype is activated in full force. It grants identity, meaning, and purpose.

But what happens when the war ends?

Jung believed that when a dominant archetype loses its relevance, it creates an identity vacuum. Without integration—without understanding that the warrior is only one part of the self—a person becomes stuck, clinging to the warrior persona long after it's useful. This leads to isolation, restlessness, and a fear of softness or vulnerability. The individual cannot transition into a new role (father, partner, citizen) because they haven't been taught how to be anything other than a warrior.

The Burnout Curve

Sustained stress injuries don't explode. They erode. Over months and years, they strip away health, patience, relationships, and the capacity for joy. The World Health Organization (WHO, 2019) formally recognizes burnout as a syndrome caused by chronic workplace stress—but for veterans, the workplace was war.

Symptoms of SSI often include:
• Emotional exhaustion
• Hyperarousal and intrusive thoughts
• Disconnection from others
• Anhedonia (loss of pleasure)
• Poor sleep and chronic pain
• Inability to tolerate boredom or stillness

Yet these symptoms are often underreported, because veterans themselves don't recognize them as pathological. They often believe that what they're experiencing is just weakness, laziness, or a failure to "adjust." In truth, they are symptoms of a body and brain calibrated for war, now struggling to function in an environment that demands softness, patience, and rest.

What's worse is that this burnout is often invisible to outsiders. Veterans may appear physically healthy, high-functioning, and even successful. But inside, they feel like they're smoldering—exhausted, on edge, and hollowed out. Their nervous system remains braced for danger, their identity fused to usefulness, their sleep fragmented by dreams of roads, gunfire, or voices that no longer exist.

Burnout is not about giving up. It's about having given everything, for too long, with too little recovery. And when your body adapts to operating in extreme conditions—combat, chaos, cortisol spikes—it no longer recognizes peace as normal.

Peace feels like failure.

The research gave it a name; my life gave it a mission. Call it sustained stress, call it injury—it didn't matter. I wasn't ready to be still, or soft, or safe. So, I leaned in. *So long as the gods gave me spring in my knees, I would keep running.* I fed the fire and followed it back into the fight.

The decision to join the MEU platoon was a testament to the allure of sustained stress and the comfort found in the chaos of war. I told myself it was duty, but really, it was the same fire—no longer hidden, now given a banner to march under. It was as if we were addicted to the adrenaline-fueled life, unable or unwilling to let go of the intense brotherhood and purpose it provided.

The prospect of returning to a mundane existence, where the biggest challenge was deciding what to eat for dinner, filled us with a sense of impending doom. We were haunted by the knowledge that no one back home could truly understand what we had endured and who we had become. The war had changed us, and we feared that the civilian world would only see our scars as flaws to be pitied or, worse, ignored.

Steel Curtain

So, we chose to remain in the crucible, seeking solace in the familiar rhythm of combat. The MEU platoon offered a new challenge, a chance to test ourselves further and prove our mettle. It was a decision born of a desire to belong, to matter, and to continue pushing ourselves beyond the limits of what most would consider sane. We were aware that our choice might be deemed foolish or even suicidal, but it was ours to make. And so, with eager hearts and minds, we embraced the path that led further into the abyss, knowing full well that it might be our undoing.

The transition was seamless, as if we had never left the battlefield. The training was rigorous and all-consuming, pushing us to our physical and mental limits. It was during these moments that I felt most alive, my senses heightened, and my purpose crystal clear. We were preparing for the unknown, readying ourselves for any challenge that awaited us. The days blurred together, each one a testament to our resilience and determination. We were forging ourselves into an unbreakable force, or so we believed. Little did we know that the true test of our strength would come not from any external threat but from the shadows of our own minds.

Following intensive pre-deployment training, our Marine Expeditionary Unit (MEU) was immediately redeployed to Iraq for Operation Steel Curtain. This significant operation involved two MEUs, one from the 1st and another from the 2nd Marine Division, positioned strategically along opposite banks of the Euphrates River. Our advance commenced at the Syrian border, progressing southward, systematically securing each town and establishing forward operating bases along the river's course, all the way to Ramadi.

Psychological operations were integral; C-130 aircraft disseminated leaflets to the riverside communities, providing prior notification of our impending arrival. I once obtained a leaflet, a small slip of paper the size of a business card, and sought translation. A stark black and white image of a Marine, helmet-clad, dominated the card, save for his eyes, which glowed a phosphorescent green, reminiscent of night vision goggles. Surrounding the portrait was Arabic text, which the interpreter rendered as a chilling warning: "The Marines who destroyed Fallujah are coming. Leave now or be destroyed."

The impact was immediate. Upon reaching the first city, a mass exodus ensued. Civilians hastily gathered meager supplies—food and water—and retreated into the unforgiving desert, awaiting our departure. For the ensuing four months, we relentlessly moved, house to house, block by block, maintaining an unrelenting operational tempo. Each night brought occupation of Iraqi homes; each dawn, continued combat operations that included house-to-house fighting, and more 500-pound bombs than I could count.

We conducted recon of the route for the infantry battalion to move into their staging positions and then left our trucks behind with the rear echelon troops. Each of the teams in the platoon attached to an infantry company. We were attached to Fox Company. Our job was to move with the troops and occupy the high rooftops providing observation reports and employing sniper fire.

Everyone was carrying extra ammo because we didn't know what we were getting into. A few blocks into the first city of the campaign an AK-47 fired at the Marines from the top windows of the local mosque. The Marines immediately returned fire. From 5 or 6 of the adjacent rooftops and from the Marines on the street. I was on the building directly adjacent, and I fired 30 to 40 rounds from my M 249 into the row of glass along the top and then stopped. I didn't see any movement.

The Marines on my left and right continued to expend the extra machine gun ammo. A gun truck moved into position on the street and started hitting the dome of the little mosque with 40mmgrenades. Finally, there was a lull in the fire, some plaster fell from the side of the mosque, and you could hear it break apart when it hit the ground. A Marine on the next rooftop over stood up and yelled, "America! Fuck Yeah!" At this, I turned and sat with my back to the wall. I looked up at the sky and thought about the absurdity of this war. Someone began firing into the Mosque again and my team leader called out, "we're moving".

We cleared the towns house by house using a grid reference guide in which each separate structure had its own letter-number designation. I could literally call an F/A-18 Hornet and have them drop a 500-pound bomb on a building by telling them it was B-23. The force that the MEU brought in terms of total firepower was massive. Any car left on the street had a rocket fired into it, out of fear that it might be a car bomb, and we breached every gate and every door everywhere we went.

House by House

After a while, the scale of destruction became routine—just another part of the day's work. And in that strange new normal, survival meant finding scraps of ordinary life wherever we could.

Early in the campaign, weary of monotonous Meals Ready-to-Eat (MREs), we began supplementing our rations with locally sourced protein: chickens, sheep, goats, even a turkey, all butchered by the Marines from the country while the city boys learned how to do it for themselves. Every dwelling yielded a bounty—ample rice, lush green onions, and tomatoes from garden yards, flatbreads, and cooking oil—we helped ourselves. It might sound like nothing, but looking back, it was telling. The fact that we could carve out moments of domesticity amid the rubble wasn't proof of resilience—it was proof of how comfortable we had become inside the chaos.

Looking back, it's clear that sustained stress injuries are born from that relentless pressure and grind of day-to-day operations, and those three deployments in 2003, 2004, and 2005 are a clear reflection of that reality for me. In the five years I had been in the Marines, almost two of them had been spent in high-threat areas.

Coming Home

Coming home early, weeks before my platoon, felt less like arriving and more like slipping out of my own skin. The war was still burning in my body, but the world around me had gone quiet. Someone in admin handed me a care package that had chased us through the mail and never caught up until now. Inside was a bottle of Crown Royal.

I started each morning with a pour from it, another before lunch, watching the level drop as if it were marking the distance between who I had been and who I was supposed to become. The chaos of Steel Curtain had collapsed overnight into paperwork, formation calls, and sterile hallways. Time warped and flattened. I knew my identity was about to change, but none of it felt real—the alcohol just made it easier to float through the days as my old life dissolved behind me.

I told myself I was choosing family, but the truth is I was just trying to choose *something*—anything solid to hold on to while the ground shifted under me. My sons had grown in my absence, strangers wearing familiar faces, and I clung to the idea that they still needed me. Leaving the Marines felt like stepping off a cliff, but staying meant vanishing completely into the war. Fatherhood became my lifeline, a story I could tell myself about who I might be on the other side of all this. I signed the papers, turned in my gear, and walked away from the only world where I had ever felt entirely at home.

I didn't know who I was without the war, without the Marines.

Homer was right—we men, despite our strength, are fragile creatures. No warrior is immune to the invisible injuries sustained through prolonged exposure to stress. Yet within Homer's bleak acknowledgment lies a subtle promise of hope: if we can bear suffering, we can also transcend it. Real strength is not in avoiding injury but in confronting it honestly and courageously.

I now understand that my sustained stress injuries are not weaknesses; they are evidence of my humanity. Acknowledging them is the first step toward genuine healing. We who have lived through chronic stress must learn a different kind of courage—the courage to be vulnerable, to ask for help, to relinquish the comforting illusion of invulnerability. Our strength must evolve into self-awareness and compassion, into acceptance and integration.

We cannot control our afflictions, but we can choose how we respond. The fire within me may never fully extinguish, but it no longer needs to consume me. Instead, it can illuminate a new path— one defined not by the pain I've endured, but by the wisdom I've gained from enduring it.

Chapter 4: Blood Memory

When Combat Etches Trauma into the Soul

"It is a hard thing for the living to behold these regions of the dead. Great rivers and terrible streams flow between us, and none may cross them while he yet lives."

— Homer, *The Odyssey*, Book XI, trans. Samuel Butler, 1898 (public domain)

It's an Injury

Traumatic Stress Injuries is the term that I use to describe what I think is commonly thought of as PTSD. That moment in time that burned a spot in the mind with such an intensity that it has the potential to become a recurring thought, complete with emotion, for the entirety of the person's life. That thought, that memory, of the day, or the time, when everything got real. The day that you almost lost your life, watched a friend lose theirs, learned that you're vulnerable to abuse by a stronger human, that day when your consciousness shifted and your identity changed.

I don't like the term PTSD, but I accept it because I know that people who don't really understand combat and the experience of a warrior are the ones making it up. And I know that they're doing the best that they can. What I don't like about it is the D for disorder. The word disorder implies that it could be put in order. Everything will be like it never happened if the person can just put their mind in order. This just isn't true. The event is more than a memory in your mind; it is a memory in your body and has become a part of all of you.

Fear as First Teacher

My first military experience that I would classify as a Traumatic Stress Injury occurred during training. I had successfully completed Marine Corps boot camp, the School of Infantry, and passed the Basic Reconnaissance Course, earning the title of Recon Man. At that point, I was in the final portion of Navy SERE school, where they put you in a simulated prison camp.

At the Navy SERE school, waterboarding was used to teach stubborn students that interrogators can and will break them if they don't provide the necessary information. I was one of those stubborn students who resisted their initial interrogation methods. My experience with waterboarding showed me that if I endured it long enough, I would eventually reveal all the information I had. If it continued, I might even begin to fabricate details or confess to things I hadn't done just to make it stop.

They had me doing mountain climbers and jumping jacks for five straight minutes to get my heart racing. I'd been sleeping outside for the last week with nothing but my uniform and a scrap of parachute cloth, and the cold had left me raw—my nose running, my skin chapped. When they finally ordered me onto the table, I peeled off my shirt with trembling hands.

They pulled the thick leather strap that crisscrossed my body from shoulders to ankles until I could barely expand my ribs to breathe. Then they flopped a soaking towel straight from a bucket of ice water onto my bare chest. I inhaled sharply pressing at the straps. A smaller towel followed, just as soaked, draped across my forehead, eyes, and nose. The cold soaked straight through my skin, numbing my muscles until they trembled without my permission.

The towel sealed over my face like a living thing, pressing me into darkness, and my chest convulsed uselessly against the strap. The water filled my sinuses, I tried to control my throat, I gagged and then coughed and lost all control, my resolve cracked, and a primal fear took hold.

I gave them my name, social, and birthdate. Then they asked other questions, and when I hesitated to answer, they poured the water into my sinuses again, and I broke, again—three more times. I gave them all the information I had by the end, and I was acutely aware of their satisfaction in breaking me after I had resisted all their other methods. They knew all along that eventually I'd break.

They got me. And what hit hardest wasn't just the fear—it was knowing how easily it had happened. I had gone in believing I could outlast them, that my will was stronger than whatever they could throw at me. But the truth was harsher: no one beats it. Everyone breaks.

As Malcolm Gladwell explains in *Talking to Strangers*, "Part of what they try to do in the Navy school is show people that you really will capitulate at some point" (Gladwell, 2019, p. 244). The Pentagon's Joint Personnel Recovery Agency, which monitored SERE programs across the branches, put it even more bluntly: "It's 100 percent effective on our students. We have never had anyone not capitulate" (Gladwell, 2019, p. 248).

Hearing that years later didn't make it easier—but it made it make sense. What I felt on that table wasn't weakness; it was what happens to everyone when the body decides survival matters more than pride.

When it was over, they made me roll off the table onto all fours. My limbs shook with exhaustion, my chest still hitching for air. The instructors spoke in an obnoxiously fake Russian accent, circling me, tossing clipped commands like I was a disobedient dog. It was surreal—being completely drained, terrified of what was still coming, and yet strangely relieved just to be off that table.

They pulled a sandbag over my head, and ordered me to crawl on all fours. I followed their boots and their voices to the back of a stake-bed truck. The metal floor rattled under me as I climbed inside. When I realized I was sitting on a bench among the other students, relief washed through me, and all I wanted was to disappear among them—to stop being noticed, to never draw that kind of attention again.

When the truck began to move, I hoped it would be a long ride.

The water board was a physical, soul-deep experience. I could feel the panic rising within me, and I knew that if it continued, I would break. I would say anything to make it stop, and the thought of confessing to lies or inventing details to end the torture became a terrifying reality.

The experience changed me. I realized that my body held the memory of that trauma, and it would forever be a part of who I was. It was a scar, a mark of that moment in time when my mortality and vulnerability were laid bare. It was a brutal initiation into a new understanding of myself and the world around me.

From that day on, I carried a different weight on my shoulders. I knew that my mind and body could be pushed to their limits and beyond, and the knowledge of that capacity for endurance was both a strength and a burden

Crossing the Line

A few months later, at the beginning of 2003, we were deployed to Kuwait, and we spent the next few weeks living in tents and then waiting on the border of Iraq, waiting to begin the invasion. An experience that blurred the lines between sustained stress and traumatic stress. Every day was like being a part of a traveling caravan of death.

If SERE had shown me how fear could take over, Iraq showed me how quickly that fear becomes a way of life.

The wait on the border was suffocating—heat, dust, and dread blending into days that felt endless. We all carried our own scars, some fresh, some long hidden, and knew that once we crossed, there was no turning back. Training and brotherhood kept us steady, but when the order finally came, we moved with the heavy knowledge that life would never return to what it was.

That night the sky lit with Tomahawks and airstrikes tearing into Iraqi defenses. Under that cover we pushed north across the desert toward Highway 1, the road to Baghdad. Our units moved in a relentless leapfrog, town by town, clearing resistance as we went, with the 1st Marine Division reinforced by the 2nd under General James Mattis driving the advance. It was war in motion—fast, brutal, and irreversible.

The First Shattering

The long hours spent driving across the southern desert lulled me into a state of disbelief and wonder. It was only when we reached Nasiriyah that the reality of the situation sunk in for me. An Army logistics unit had taken a wrong turn off Highway 1 and arrived in Nasiriyah ahead of the Marines. As we advanced toward the bridge, we passed the remnants of their trucks and equipment. They had been completely scavenged, turned over with axles, wheels, and suspensions looted. Blood smears and handprints were visible on some of the vehicles.

As the Marines took their positions along the riverbanks on either side of the bridge, the shooting began. Enemy fire was coming from across the river on the north side. In an attempt to recover the members of the captured Army unit, infantry Marines had crossed the bridge in their amphibious armored personnel carriers (AAVs), but some of them were destroyed by enemy RPG fire. Their smoking hulls were barely visible on the other side of the river. The remainder of their unit had retreated south of the bridge just as we were arriving.

The Marines established a defensive perimeter upon stopping, ensuring 360-degree security. The Marines positioned on the river side of the perimeter were engaging the enemy with increasing fire while simultaneously constructing defensive positions.

I was on the opposite side of the perimeter, looking back the way we had come and listening to the escalating gunfire when a loud explosion occurred nearby, and a piece of shrapnel landed in the back of the truck with me bouncing off the floor and taking a chunk out of the wooden chest that doubled as storage for our NVGs and spare radio parts. I stared at its jagged edges, and thought about what it would have done to my flesh.

Realizing that I was more vulnerable in the open back truck than I was effective, I got out and took cover by the front wheel. It didn't feel much safer there either and I couldn't see what was going on, so after a few moments on the ground I got back up behind my gun.

The intensity of the firefight increased as two pairs of Marine helicopters arrived. The Cobras and Huey's flew high into the air above the north bank of the river and then dove down to execute rocket and gun runs on the buildings along that bank.

The marines pounded the north bank of the river, and during the night, they crossed the bridge. Beneath the pre-dawn sky, painted in violets and deep blues, we rolled slowly across the bridge. On the opposite bank lay fields of garbage, with shallow canals filled with black water. I could see the infantry marines, ordered to crawl through the muck, setting up a perimeter at the far edge of the fields where the buildings began.

The stench from the garbage fields was overwhelming, and I didn't envy the marines who were lying in it, using the larger piles for cover. We drove through the morning and into the afternoon, with occasional desert rain sprinkling down on us. I was fascinated with the people I was seeing. The kids would all run out and yell "good Bush, good Bush" and hold their thumbs up.

Dissociation and Return

After leaving Nasiriyah, we moved north through the farmlands. In the evening, we entered the town of Gharraf, where we were ambushed from the windows of the buildings as we traveled in column down the main street.

I had once again been lulled into a sense of wonder at the beauty of my surroundings. The women working in the fields, adorned with brightly colored scarves, and the tall wheat grass swaying in the wind created a picture-perfect scene. I had failed to recognize what would later become telltale signs of a coming fight. People leaving. As we entered Gharraf, my truck was the second to last in the convoy when the call came over the radio: "Contact right!" My team leader shouted, "Here we go!"

Muzzle flashes strobed from the darkened windows not twenty yards away, and something in me shifted. The world narrowed to movement and noise. Something came up from the inside of my body and took over while I watched from behind my eyes: unhooking the machine gun from the T&E lock, swinging it toward the buildings, and pressing the trigger down with my thumbs. The MK 19 bucked under my hands, launching 40mm grenades into the structures beside my platoon. I emptied the first can of grenades in a single, sustained burst that tore a building apart as we drove past.

I reloaded with the second can and fired again in shorter bursts as we pushed through town. By the time we reached the edge, the second can was gone. When I began loading the third, the gun jammed—bolt locked to the rear. I stood behind it, frozen for a beat, heart hammering, ears ringing. My platoon sergeant's voice cut through the chaos, calm but urgent: he needed me to get my weapon functioning immediately.

That snapped me back. I suddenly felt the heat radiating off the weapon, the sting of grit on my face, the smell of burnt powder and grease. My hands were steady, almost eerily so, as I pulled my Leatherman from my belt. I pressed my chest against the machine gun handles to hold the spring in place and punched out the rear pin. Carefully, I bled off the tension on the bolt and removed it. I smeared the last of the grease along its length, slid it back in, and locked it down.

As we drove away from the ambush site and into a field to reorganize, my eyes felt pinned open, my throat bone dry. My teammates were laughing and hugging me, slapping my helmet, their adrenaline spilling out as shaky laughter. I didn't know how to take it. I just sat there staring ahead, silent, still locked in shock.

Night fell, and later we were ambushed again at another bridge. This time I couldn't use the MK 19 in the dark because I had no way to aim it, but I did have an infrared (IR) scope on my M 249. Through the glowing green lens I could see them kneeling behind trees. I moved quickly and fired three to five round bursts as accurately as I could.

During the fight, my team leader was shot in the foot, and we later discovered our truck was riddled with bullet holes—including one directly in front of the driver's face on the windshield. It's a mystery how more of us didn't get hit.

By morning, the adrenaline had cooled, and we were retelling the night like a campfire story. Our team leader had been medevac'd out, and now that we knew he was going to be fine, the fear had drained out of the room. One Marine laughed as he admitted he hadn't known where the fire was coming from, so he'd curled behind the front tire and just fired over the hood blindly. We started calling it the "combat curl." For the first time, I felt a flicker of that strange relief-laughter too—the kind that only comes when you realize you're still alive.

We examined the men who had ambushed us before moving on. They were dressed in civilian clothing—blue jeans, jackets, track suits, and running shoes—and were armed with RPGs, hand grenades, and ammunition stuffed in their pockets. They had identification cards, and our interpreter informed us they were from Saudi Arabia, Syria, and other places. None of them were Iraqi.

Every day following that moment is a blur of gunfights, dead bodies, and destruction. The landscape was a nightmare, with oil fires burning in every direction while the population descended into chaos. People looted and burned everything that once belonged to the government. Packs of wild dogs ate from piles of human corpses. There was no power on the electrical lines, the sanitation systems were malfunctioning, and the streets filled with sewage and uncollected garbage.

Saddam had opened the doors to the prisons, releasing all the criminals into the public. They joined forces with foreign fighters, forming guerrilla units that employed increasingly cunning tactics to ambush the military. At one point, General Mattis changed the rules of engagement to "if you feel threatened, destroy it," as Marines were frequently ambushed by what they believed were civilians.

After that day, we experienced much more fighting while staying on the move. When I reflect on that experience, it's a blur of images accompanied by emotions of fear and desire. I know that the experience changed me profoundly. I had never had an out-of-body experience before that day, and I never felt the same sense of wonder at my surroundings again. I realized I could never again be lulled into a sense of safety. The enemy lay in wait in the shadows, and I knew he was there—even if he wasn't. After that day, I became a man ready to fight, to kill, and to die at any moment. In fact, I felt as if I were searching for that opportunity.

Images That Don't Leave

The following year, we returned to Iraq to fight in Fallujah, and I had an experience that has remained etched in my memory with such intensity that even twenty years later, I still dream about that day. The images are vivid in my mind, accompanied by a mix of fear and a desire to fight.

We were ambushed from a ditch alongside the road. We had trained for this situation, and instead of running when we were ambushed, we were prepared to stop and fight. That day, we lost our platoon commander and more than half a dozen other men were wounded. My friend lost his hands when an RPG hit his truck. The fight lasted most of the afternoon, and after we watched the medevacs fly away and successfully chased the enemy from the battlefield, we were ordered to collect the enemy dead and load them onto our trucks to bring back to base.

The gunfights I was used to, but I had never handled dead human bodies before that day. One of the men that we had to put on the hood of our truck had a head wound, I had shot him in the face at close range, and when we loaded him on the hood of the truck his skull fell apart.

His brain rolled out of his head, part of it remaining on the hood and part of it falling onto the ground. For a long moment I just stared, I'm not sure why, but I thought the brain matter looked like a scoop of raspberry sherbet melting in the hot sun.

During the drive back to base, from my seat in the front passenger side of the truck I could see the back side of the man's sinuses and eyeballs, the missing piece of skull hung by a flap of scalp. The other man that we had put on the hood of the truck, his sweatpants had been caught in the concertina wire we kept on the hood and his pants were down around his thighs.

For a half hour, while we drove back to base, I stared at the grotesque combination of naked male genitals and the vision of what the back side of the human face looks like. That drive back to base didn't end when we parked. Part of me stayed in that cab, staring at what we had carried.

Now, simply butchering an animal or witnessing a child drop their ice cream can trigger flashbacks that pull my thoughts into the past, along with a wave of emotions. I experience conflicting and paradoxical feelings of fear and a desire to fight, which cause my body to tense up. This can occur even on a beautiful day surrounded by people that I love. I don't want to ruin their day by sharing my inner thoughts; those close to me have no idea that while we talk, laugh, and listen to the children play, I might be fighting back the feelings of despair and the desire to destroy.

What the Body Remembers

What happened to me didn't just leave a mark in my memory—it burned itself into my nervous system. And I'm not the only one. Countless veterans walk around with similar wounds, invisible to the eye but etched into the body like a second skin. It's not all in our heads—it's in our hearts, our guts, our muscles, our blood. That's not poetic exaggeration. That's science.

Dr. Bessel van der Kolk, a trauma specialist and author of *The Body Keeps the Score*, explains it like this: trauma isn't just something you remember—it's something you relive, over and over, in the body. You smell something. You hear a sound. You see a kid drop an ice cream cone, and suddenly your whole-body tenses like it's back in Iraq. You don't choose it. It chooses you. It bypasses your thinking brain entirely. That's because trauma shifts control from the rational prefrontal cortex to the more primitive parts of your brain—the amygdala, the hippocampus, and the brainstem. Fight, flight, freeze. That's where trauma lives (van der Kolk, 2014).

And here's the kicker—those changes aren't temporary. They leave lasting effects. Studies show that people with severe trauma, especially repeated combat trauma, show hyperactive amygdalas (which means you're always on edge), shrunken hippocampi (which screws up your sense of time and memory), and underactive prefrontal cortices (so you can't just logic your way out of it) (Yehuda & LeDoux, 2007). Your brain literally reorganizes itself around the trauma.

Archetypes, Initiation, and the Underworld

Carl Jung talked about how warriors often undergo a kind of descent into the underworld—a spiritual death and rebirth. But here's the problem: no one teaches you how to come back. No one welcomes you home. So instead of being reborn, you just stay in the dark. Jung said we all have a shadow, and if we don't face it consciously, it eats us alive.

In combat, we meet the shadow directly. We meet it in ourselves when we feel the desire to kill. We meet it in others when they try to kill us. That shadow isn't evil—it's part of us. But if we don't integrate it—if we don't find a way to give it shape, to speak about it, to understand it—it controls us. That's what trauma does. It silences the warrior. And the only way back is through storytelling, through ritual, through reconnection with life and meaning.

Back to Blood Memory

Homer's depiction of battle is visceral, vivid, and brutal—not a distant, glorified image but a raw snapshot of violence, confusion, and death. His words capture the chaotic intensity of combat, where life and death dance so closely they become indistinguishable. Reading Homer now, after my experiences, I understand his words differently. He was not merely describing an event; he was capturing a transformation—the exact moment when trauma is etched irrevocably into a warrior's soul.

In combat, life is reduced to its starkest elements—movement, sound, sensation. A sword rises, an axe whirls, bodies spin lifelessly. These sensory snapshots aren't just witnessed; they're absorbed into the deepest fibers of a warrior's being. Homer understood intuitively what modern neuroscience confirms: that trauma is more than memory; it's a physical and spiritual engraving. Combat changes the wiring of the brain, alters the chemistry of the body, and reshapes the landscape of identity forever.

My first encounter with this engraving came at SERE school, where waterboarding burned a primal fear into my body and forced me to face my own fragility. In Nasiriyah, that scar deepened—shrapnel striking nearby as I stood exposed in a truck bed, my body taking over, instincts rewiring themselves for survival.

In Gharraf, ambushed and firing mechanically, I floated above myself in dissociation, returning only as I forced a jammed weapon back into service. By Fallujah, trauma was my default state, seared into me by handling the bodies of men I had killed—grotesque images that still intrude decades later, triggered by something as small as blood, butchered meat, or a child dropping ice cream.

The term PTSD, with its clinical neatness and implication of disorder, always felt inadequate. It implied a linearity—trauma occurs, trauma is treated, normalcy returns. But what Homer implicitly understood—and what my experiences taught me explicitly—is that combat trauma isn't something you simply move past. It is a fundamental reordering of identity, a transformation etched into the body, spirit, and mind. The trauma I carry is not a disorder to fix; it is an injury I must integrate, a wound that shapes my very existence.

Carl Jung believed warriors descend into an underworld from which many never fully return. Homer's imagery aligns perfectly with this idea: the battle is an underworld, a place of death and chaos from which warriors emerge changed, if they emerge at all. Jung's shadow is precisely what I encountered: the capacity for violence, rage, and destruction residing within me, triggered by trauma.

Without integrating this shadow, without consciously recognizing and accepting its existence, I risked being forever controlled by it. The shadow of combat trauma must be acknowledged, understood, and integrated into a new, holistic identity—one that encompasses the warrior but is not defined solely by him.

The physiological insights of van der Kolk and Judith offer further depth. Trauma's impact isn't metaphorical—it's neurobiological, energetic, and embodied. The hyperactive amygdala, shrunken hippocampus, altered brainstem responses—these aren't abstract concepts; they're lived realities. Combat reshaped my body's architecture, embedding trauma deep within my tissues, my muscles, my blood memory. To heal isn't to forget or erase; it is to understand and integrate. The trauma remains, but my relationship to it can change.

Homer captures the chaos and brutality of combat in poetic clarity, providing a timeless mirror to my own experiences. Bodies spinning, swords rising, axes whirling—this imagery is not just historical detail;

it is eternal truth. Combat trauma is not just memory—it's blood memory, written deep within the soul, impossible to erase but possible to carry with dignity and awareness.

We warriors who survive combat carry Homer's battle within us always. Our trauma becomes a silent companion, a profound injury that shapes who we are. But it also offers an opportunity for profound self-awareness, spiritual growth, and ultimately, healing. Trauma becomes the fire that tempers our souls, forging within us not just survivors, but warriors capable of compassion, wisdom, and genuine connection.

And perhaps, in the act of acknowledging and integrating our trauma, we finally reclaim our humanity from the chaos that once sought to erase it.

Chapter 5: The Weight of Wrong

When Duty Demands What the Soul Cannot Bear

"So even in death he remembered his anger because of the armor. Thus, I know the pain of wrongs not paid, and my heart is sick with grief."

— Homer, *The Odyssey*, Book XI, trans. A.T. Murray, 1919 (public domain, adapted)

What We Did vs. Who We Are

War does not only break bodies; it breaks beliefs. Long after the smoke clears and the medals are tucked away, many veterans carry a deeper wound—a tear in the very fabric of who they are and what they believe is right. This chapter confronts the invisible injury known as *moral injury*—a soul-deep rupture caused by actions, inactions, or events that betray a person's deeply held moral code. For combat veterans like me, the wounds of war often stem not from being shot at, but from being forced to live with what we saw, what we did, and what we could not stop.

What Moral Injury Is

Moral injury is not officially classified as a medical diagnosis like PTSD, yet its effects can be just as devastating. Researchers such as Dr. Brett Litz have described it as "the lasting psychological, biological, spiritual, behavioral and social impact of perpetrating, failing to prevent, or bearing witness to acts that transgress deeply held moral beliefs and expectations." (Litz et al., 2009) Unlike PTSD, which is rooted in fear, moral injury is rooted in guilt, shame, and betrayal. These feelings can linger in silence, buried beneath layers of denial and duty, until life's pressures crack open the vault.

During the invasion of Iraq and my later deployments, I bore witness to the slaughter of innocents, the deaths of children, the silent aftermath of air strikes, and the cold logic of military decisions made far above my pay grade. I was told to say nothing, to keep moving, to trust that what we were doing was right. These memories weren't just images; they became burdens, each one heavier than the last.

Moral injury is a form of soul-wounding that results when one's moral compass is violated in the extreme environments of war. While training prepares the body for combat, nothing prepares the conscience for its aftermath. This chapter explores how witnessing and surviving these moments of moral dissonance plants a kind of rot in the heart of a warrior—a rot that grows in silence, infecting self-worth, relationships, faith, and the very will to live.

Confessions in the Shadows

In the conversations that I have had with my fellow combat veterans I have noticed that the last stories to get told, the stories that hide until a trust has been established, are the stories of moral injury. Because I was always willing to share my own stories of moral injuries with other combat veterans, I inspired them to share theirs with me. Sometimes what I heard made me feel uncomfortable.

I've heard confessions that still echo in my head. One man told me how his commander ordered him to shoot a woman approaching a checkpoint because they believed she wore a suicide vest. He obeyed—and only after she fell did they discover she was a pregnant mother and not a terrorist.

I've heard about prisoners blindfolded, beaten and thrown from the back of 7-ton trucks. I've heard about farmers shot in their fields because someone thought the shovel in their hands was burying an IED instead of turning over the soil. And so many like my own of the unintentional killing of children with bombs and stray bullets.

My first experience was watching a captain in my battalion call in a 500-pound bomb from an F/A 18 on a exhaust pipe he was mistaking for an enemy mortar. The exhaust pipe on an irrigation pump that was supplying water to a small village that I had been watching in my bino's for a half an hour. Women, children, goats and donkeys, they vanished in dust seconds after the fighter jet could be heard coming toward earth.

What all these stories shared wasn't just violence—it was what happens when people are handed absolute power over others and quietly assured there will be no consequences. War doesn't just strip away fear; it erodes restraint. When cruelty becomes easy and punishment unlikely, some men descend into it—and the rest of us are left carrying what we saw them become.

These weren't war stories told for bravado. They were whispered late at night, voices cracked with regret, often followed by silence and an awkward tension. They weren't about fear of dying. They were about crossing lines you never imagined you could approach and realizing you can never go back.

These confessions, spoken in hushed voices or behind the cover of alcohol and exhaustion, reveal a kind of wound that never fully heals. What haunts these men is not just what they did—but what they were told it meant. They were sent to war in the name of freedom, justice, and protection, but what many of us witnessed on the ground didn't match those ideals. Instead, we saw profit-motivated policies, civilian casualties, and operational decisions that favored political optics over human life.

And sometimes, the smallest acts revealed how deeply that dehumanization had seeped in.

In 2004, during our time in Fallujah, we conducted dozens of late-night raids on suspected fighters and bomb makers. Before they were transferred to Abu Ghraib prison, detainees were held in a makeshift facility—a deep ditch about eight feet down, divided into cells by heavy gates, with concertina wire stretched across the top to keep them from climbing out.

One afternoon, while we were gearing up for patrol, I watched a Marine tasked with feeding them toss their plates through the wire so they would land in the dirt. The men would have to pick their food out of the dust like animals. I knew we had put four men in there the night before. Something about it hit me wrong. I went to the chow hall, got four to-go plates, and carried them over. I dropped to my hands and knees and slid the meals gently through the wire as their hands reached up to take them. They called out to me—not in words I understood, but the tone said enough. They were grateful.

I'm not sure why I did it. Most guys just chose to hate our enemy. But I couldn't. It already felt wrong that we had them in a hole, in the sun, under wire—and then to make them eat out of the dirt? A few months after the end of that deployment, when the Abu Ghraib scandal broke and the images of naked men being harassed and degraded by Americans filled the news, I felt sick. Humiliated. I had helped put some of those men in that prison. To see what they endured at the end of it made me ashamed—not of my service, but of what we had allowed ourselves to become.

That shame—the realization that good men can be made cruel—was its own kind of wound.

This betrayal of our moral compass compounds the trauma. It is not just that we committed acts we never imagined ourselves capable of, but that we did so under a false banner. No one named that betrayal more bluntly than Smedley Butler.

A Two-Time Hero Who Refused the Medal Game

Major General Smedley D. Butler—one of the most decorated Marines in U.S. history, and one of only two men ever awarded the Medal of Honor twice—delivered *War Is a Racket* after retiring, exposing the profit engine behind American wars. Having fought from the Philippines and China to Haiti and World War I, he came to believe war served business more than freedom. In his speech, he even mocked the "medal game," admitting that the honors pinned to his chest were part of the system that keeps young men fighting.

His confession was devastating in its honesty: "I spent thirty-three years and four months in active military service... and during that period I spent most of my time being a high-class muscle man for Big Business, for Wall Street, and for the bankers... I helped make Mexico safe for American oil interests, helped make Haiti and Cuba a decent place for the National City Bank boys to collect revenues... helped purify Nicaragua for the international banking house of Brown Brothers... brought light to the Dominican Republic for the American sugar interests... helped make Honduras 'right' for the American fruit companies."

It reads like a moral autopsy. The anger is political, but the wound is personal: the realization that honor and service were leveraged for exploitation. That is moral injury in plain sight.

What makes Butler's speech compelling is not just its critique of war profiteering, but the emotional urgency behind it. He wasn't a pacifist by nature—he had lived as a warrior. His anger toward the system that used him may have also been anger toward himself for playing the part.

This is one of the most painful aspects of moral injury: realizing that you not only witnessed injustice, but may have personally carried it out. Butler's transformation—from decorated Marine to outspoken whistleblower—was not just political. It was spiritual and moral. He was reclaiming his conscience, possibly seeking redemption by exposing the truth and preventing others from becoming pawns in the same deadly game.

Seen through the lens of moral injury, *War Is a Racket* is more than an anti-war pamphlet—it is an act of moral reckoning. Butler used his platform to name the corruption, to acknowledge the betrayal of the ideals he once served, and to advocate for change. His voice carries the weight of lived experience, the burden of knowing, and the courage to speak. For veterans today who struggle with similar feelings of betrayal, guilt, and disillusionment, Butler's words still resonate. They remind us that moral injury is not weakness—it is the soul's refusal to be silenced by injustice.

When Validation Hollows You Out

When I found *War Is a Racket*, sometime in 2011, it made me feel understood. I realized I wasn't alone. I wasn't crazy. The hypocrisy I sensed in the wars had already been exposed by someone who wore the same uniform, someone far more decorated, far more revered. Major General Smedley Butler had seen behind the curtain too—and he'd named what he found. His words validated everything I had wrestled with, the sense of betrayal, the guilt, the gnawing disillusionment.

But along with that validation came something heavier—a kind of existential apathy. If a man like Butler, with two Medals of Honor and a platform to speak the truth, couldn't wake the nation a hundred years ago, what chance do the rest of us have now? If his warnings were forgotten and the machine kept rolling—if the racket still thrives—then what real difference can any of us make? That realization didn't inspire me. It hollowed me out.

Indistinguishable Enemy, Indiscriminate Cost

In 2003 during the invasion of Iraq I was involved in a running series of engagements with men that were indistinguishable from the other civilians around them, except that they held a rifle, a shovel, a cell phone and or binoculars. They planted 155mm artillery shells in the sides of roads and waited in a nearby ditch with the ends of the blasting wire and a battery. They fired rockets from the backs of dump trucks and lobbed 60mm mortars escaping on the back of motorcycles. They used every tactic in the guerrilla fighter handbook.

These tactics inevitably frustrate uniformed troops, because they rarely know who the enemy is—while the enemy always knows who they are. During contact—when the shooting starts—insurgents in plain clothes blend into the chaos, and fear takes over. Soldiers fire at movement, and at what the others are firing at. The battlefield becomes a blur of confusion and adrenaline. Often, no one ever knows exactly what happened.

At the beginning of my second deployment I had seen much civilian death before, but I had never been close enough to touch the dead civilians, never been startled by the raw, intimate horror of it—until Fallujah, 2004.

Fallujah: The Field of Blankets

The morning was already hot when we entered the village. Twenty-five Marines moved through the palm grove, spread out in a deliberate line. I was on the far right, walking a small irrigation ditch, eyes scanning the mud-brick homes ahead. The dogs started barking first, followed by the curious, wary eyes of villagers who had survived a night of fire. It was supposed to be a cleanup operation—a battle damage assessment. The real fight had happened hours earlier, guided by the thermal eyes of an AC-130 gunship in the pitch black of a moonless Iraqi night.

As we moved closer, life had resumed in subtle ways. A woman in a vibrant dress and canary-yellow scarf was baking flatbread for her family. Her defiance caught my attention. She didn't look up at me as I passed, but I felt the weight of her dignity. After a night of bullets and death, she had stepped out barefoot to feed her loved ones. That moment etched itself into my mind—not just for her courage, but for what it masked: the quiet, resolved endurance of people living under siege.

We expected to find weapons, enemy dead, or wounded fighters. But I found blankets—laid gently across the field, too neatly placed to ignore. I approached the first one, nervous it might be rigged with explosive. I knelt and lifted the edge, and underneath was a little girl. Maybe, four years old. Long hair, black curls. A white dress with little flowers. Her thigh a bloody stump draining into a dark puddle in the dirt, blood on the hem of her dress. Her severed leg placed next to her. Her eyes didn't follow me. They stared upward into the sky, unblinking.

As I stood, more blankets came into view. One, then another, then another. A whole field of them. Children. I didn't count. I couldn't. My knees ached; my breath caught in my throat. John, my teammate, arrived as I turned away.

"Did they find a weapons cache?" I asked.

"Nothing," he said. "But there are over a hundred wounded at the village elder's house—mostly women and kids."

My stomach knotted up and I doubled over in pain, the girls image vivid in my mind's eye.

When I stood back up John asked. "You good?"

"No… those blankets are covering little kids." I said, as I noticed, the holes in the roof and walls of the nearest house. As my eyes scanned over the area, my imagination could see the children run out of the house into the dark, the machine guns in the AC-130 chasing their heat signatures, cutting them down before they could get away and, then their family members came out and placed blankets over them until they could come back and bury them.

Later that day, we loaded wounded children into our gun trucks. I watched a man cradle his daughter, holding her belly closed with his bare hands. The girl's eyes fluttered. No screaming. No crying. Just quiet surrender. We drove them to a hospital; no words exchanged between us. The father looked into my eyes with something I still can't define—not hate, not forgiveness, just a raw, human truth.

The deployment to Fallujah in 2004 was a turning point in my thinking and character. At the beginning of our deployment, we fought to secure the city of Fallujah. After weeks of intense fighting, we were ordered to evacuate the city. Over the next four months, especially toward the end of our deployment, we reported that the inhabitants of Fallujah were fortifying the city. From the outskirts, we watched as they used bulldozers to barricade streets and buildings. They placed IEDs, constructed fighting positions, and prepared to defend the city.

As we monitored and reported on these developments, we struggled with the reality that we had already taken the city and then turned it back over to them, knowing we would have to take it again. At the end of the summer, the 2nd Marines replaced us in the city. A few weeks after our departure, Operation Phantom Fury began. It became the bloodiest battle American troops had faced since the Battle of Hue, Vietnam in 1968.

We had already taken the city once, and for months, we had reported to higher command that it was being fortified after we relinquished control. Watching the command send in the 2nd Marines, knowing the city had been fortified, felt like betrayal. I could no longer convince myself that our superiors or the government cared about the lives of young Marines. The line from the movie *Full Metal Jacket*— "Marines die; that's what we're here for"—seemed more like reality than fiction.

This deployment marked the beginning of my disillusionment with our country and its wars. I started questioning the official narratives and began to doubt the patriotic rhetoric I had once embraced. I started to see the wars as driven by big business and understood that we were being sacrificed for the profit margins of major corporations.

Years later, the little girl under the blanket would show up in my thoughts at the most inappropriate times, eyes motionless. One time, I was attending a group guided meditation, "leaves on the stream," at the Vet Center. In my mind's eye I imagined a stream with leaves floating on it, and then I noticed the little girl standing on her one leg on the opposite bank of the stream, staring at me. She was in my meditation. I tried to control my breath, to remain calm, but eventually I failed. My breathing was rapid and heavy; I was panicking. Embarrassed, I stood up and walked out as fast as I could.

Moral injury isn't only born in the blast. Sometimes it arrives in the silence after, when the system moves on and leaves the living behind to make sense of what it used them for.

I had seen dead children before Afghanistan—tiny bodies in the rubble of Iraq, villages silenced mid-breath. Those images never left. But Kabul was different. Not because the children there were spared death, but because they were made to survive it.

I didn't see one boy. I saw a system—toddlers in sackcloth shaking coffee cans like ledgers, little girls moving in barefoot packs, a tiny tissue-seller who finally broke under the rejection, threw a screaming fit and then obeyed hunger's physics to try the next car. It wasn't "poverty" I was watching; it was an economy of survival where childhood was the collateral. Their coffee cans weren't props; they were books kept in public view. The flatbread wasn't charity; it was a receipt stamped paid through sunset.

That was when I understood that moral injury doesn't always come from the blast itself. Sometimes it comes later, when you see the machine still turning, children feeding its gears with the only thing they have left—their lives. The ledger wasn't abstract anymore. It had hair and dust and small hands.

Twenty, One Year Wars

Once, sitting in a vehicle on the tarmac waiting to pick up VIPs, I talked with a staff officer—a 27-year SEAL who said he'd survived trial on seven murder charges for actions in combat. Staffers rarely went outside the wire, but this one had the look of someone who still knew how to break things.

He told me something that stuck. He said, "It's been eighteen one-year wars."
Then he explained: "When a new case officer comes in, it takes them three months just to learn the gates, the schedule, the systems. Another three months before they can produce anything good. By month nine they might have a few real relationships. At twelve

months they leave, never to return. The same with the military—new guys come in, occupy, then leave. Maybe someone replaces them, maybe not. But the relationships always get severed."

That's what the machine does: it forgets.
It chews through time and people like they're interchangeable, erasing bonds as soon as they're formed. Every rotation resets the clock, wipes the slate, makes the losses seem like they never happened. Until you look up and realize it's not one twenty-year war you've been fighting—it's twenty first years, stacked on top of bones.

As Afghanistan fell, that same ledger came due again.
One of my beta readers—a veteran who had fought there—told me the hardest part wasn't what happened in combat, but watching how we left. He said he cried watching the withdrawal on TV. Said it felt like watching friends die all over again, only slower this time, under the weight of our silence.

I understood what he meant.
I had interpreters who had walked beside American soldiers since they were teenagers, kids with notebooks and borrowed boots who grew into men running missions with SOF and CIA teams. They had risked everything—family, country, future—to stand with us.

And then we left them on the tarmac, the same way the machine leaves everyone once it's done taking what it came for. The machine taught them to survive, then left them to die—proof that it was never built to protect life, only to consume it.

Long after the battlefield falls silent, moral injury continues its campaign within. Unlike physical wounds, there are no scars to show for it, only a gnawing ache—an unbearable weight pressed into the soul. It can isolate a man, drive him to drink, or push him to the edge. But there is also power in naming it, in pulling the demon from the shadows. Moral injury may never vanish, but it can be carried with honesty, integrated with meaning. And perhaps, in time, it can even become a reason to live—to speak, to warn, to guide others away from the same dark path.

Of all the demons that live inside a combat veteran, moral injury is the most insidious. It wears many faces and takes many forms—shame, guilt, betrayal, regret. Unlike physical wounds, moral injury often remains hidden, festering deep in the soul. It is the final burden to descend upon a war-weary veteran, arriving when the rest of life begins to unravel—when relationships break, when hope fades, when the weight of it all becomes too much to bear. That's when moral injury strikes hardest, not as a memory, but as a judgment. Not as a scar, but as a wound that never truly heals.

Moral injury is not a disorder. It's not a diagnosis you can check off on a clipboard. It's not even officially recognized in the Diagnostic and Statistical Manual of Mental Disorders (DSM-5). And yet, for many of us who have come home from war, it's the single most defining injury we carry.

Unlike PTSD, which is rooted in fear—the fear of dying, the fear of pain—moral injury is rooted in violation. It's about shame, guilt, betrayal. It's about doing something, or witnessing something, that breaks you at the level of your conscience. It's when you can't square who you are with what you've done, what you've seen, or what you were forced to allow.

Dr. Jonathan Shay, a VA psychiatrist and author of *Achilles in Vietnam* and *Odysseus in America*, was one of the first to give this invisible wound a name. Drawing on both ancient texts and clinical experience, Shay recognized that what destroyed many Vietnam veterans wasn't the trauma of combat alone—it was the betrayal of what they believed to be right and just. Shay defines moral injury simply as "a betrayal of what's right by someone who holds legitimate authority in a high-stakes situation" (Shay, 1994; Shay, 2002) That betrayal—whether it's a commander ordering something unconscionable or a system covering up a civilian massacre—cuts deeper than bullets.

In *Achilles in Vietnam*, Shay parallels the myth of Achilles—furious, grieving, disillusioned—with the experience of modern combat veterans. Achilles watches his best friend Patroclus die due to a chain of command failure. In his rage, he desecrates the body of Hector. Then, he's left hollow.

This is what moral injury looks like. And it doesn't just sit in the brain. It sits in the soul.

What makes it worse is that so few people talk about it. We're allowed to say we have PTSD. There's a script for that. People expect you to say, "I have nightmares" or "I flinch when I hear fireworks." But how do you tell someone, "I feel like a monster because I pulled the trigger," or, "I watched a child die and didn't stop it," or, "I was used like a pawn in a war I no longer believe in"?

That's the kind of thing that eats you alive in silence. And silence is its fuel.

Dr. Bessel van der Kolk, in *The Body Keeps the Score*, speaks directly to this. He writes that trauma is not just stored in our thoughts—it lives in our bodies. "Trauma is not the story of something that happened back then," he says, "but the current imprint of that pain, horror, and fear living inside people." (van der Kolk, 2014) With moral injury, that imprint often shows up not as terror but as disgust—at yourself, at the world, at God. You may try to suppress it, but your body remembers. You flinch at kindness. You feel hollow when others laugh. You tense up because something inside you flashes to a dead little girl, lying under a blanket.

And here's where it gets even harder: moral injury is often wrapped up in what Gabor Maté calls the "myth of normal." Society wants to label us as disordered so it can keep pretending that everything else is fine. But what if we're not sick—what if we're responding appropriately to a sick system? In *The Myth of Normal*, Maté challenges the idea that trauma is just a personal problem. He says that trauma always happens in context—and that healing must, too. When we're taught that violence is noble, that sacrifice is honorable, but then we're left holding the weight of senseless death and betrayal, the injury isn't just moral—it's existential. (Maté, 2022)

We're not just wounded by what we did—we're wounded by what it meant.

Many veterans who carry moral injury report symptoms that look like depression, but with a deeper twist: feelings of worthlessness, existential emptiness, spiritual despair. They may withdraw from loved ones, lose interest in things they used to love, or feel detached from their faith. Others develop a kind of nihilistic armor. They shut down emotionally because they believe they're no longer worthy of love, peace, or joy. In severe cases, this despair leads to suicidal ideation—not because the veteran fears pain, but because they believe they deserve it.

That's how dangerous moral injury can be. Not just because it hurts, but because it convinces you that you *should* be hurting. That you *ought* to be punished. That you're broken beyond repair.

What I've come to understand—and what I want others to know—is that healing from moral injury isn't about pretending it didn't happen. It's not about "getting over it." You don't forget a field of dead children. You don't undo the acts you committed in war. What you *can* do, though, is reclaim your story. You can stop hiding. You can speak. And in doing so, you can begin to live again.

Odysseus, after years of war, doesn't come home the same man. He wanders, lies, hides who he is. But eventually, he returns—not just to his home, but to himself. That's the journey we're on. Not back to who we were before, but forward to who we're becoming. Wounded, yes. Changed, absolutely. But not lost.

"So even in death he remembered his anger because of the armor." (Homer, *Odyssey* XI, trans. Murray, 1919, public domain) When Odysseus tried to reconcile with Ajax in the underworld, Ajax turned away, unable to forgive. In those few lines Homer captured two kinds of wounds that reach beyond the battlefield: Odysseus bearing the guilt of survival and the burden of choices that left comrades dead, and Ajax consumed by shame and betrayal, so deep it followed him into death.

This is the essence of moral injury—not just fear or grief, but the fracture of trust, the unpaid debt, and the gnawing knowledge that some wrongs can never be set right. Like Odysseus, returning warriors today carry more than the visible scars of battle. We bear moral wounds—hidden, silent, heavy. What we've done or witnessed often conflicts irreconcilably with who we believed ourselves to be. The children beneath blankets in Fallujah, the father's quiet, desperate grief, and the decisions of leaders willing to trade human lives for political convenience—these images represent debts we carry, wrongs that feel permanently unpaid.

Moral injury is uniquely devastating precisely because it strikes at our deepest sense of humanity, justice, and honor. Homer understood this intuitively, long before psychology gave it a name. He recognized that grief isn't just sorrow over lost companions—it's the pain of knowing that innocence, morality, and integrity have also been casualties. My journey through war was similarly marked by this realization: the knowledge that wrongs had been committed under my watch, and that no medal, promotion, or praise could absolve the inner judgment that followed.

General Smedley Butler's moral reckoning mirrors Odysseus's grief—the agony of waking to the painful truth behind the heroic myths. Butler's recognition that war had betrayed his ideals was an act of reclaiming his soul, of attempting to repay those moral debts by exposing the truth. Yet, as Homer's verse reminds us, some wrongs linger, unpaid not through lack of courage, but simply because they are too vast, too profound to be neatly resolved.

I've learned that moral injury isn't healed by rationalizing or forgetting—it is healed by facing it honestly, by speaking openly, by refusing to be complicit in the silence that allows injustice to flourish. Like Odysseus, we who bear moral injuries must return not just to our physical homes, but to ourselves. The path back isn't through denial, but through a courageous acceptance of what has happened and a determined commitment to living with integrity despite it.

My heart may always remain, as Homer wrote, "sick with grief." Some burdens cannot be fully set down; they become part of us, shaping how we move through the world. But grief acknowledged, debts openly named, and stories honestly told transform moral injury from silent despair into moral courage. The heaviness doesn't vanish, but it becomes bearable—something carried openly, shared with those who understand its weight.

In the end, Homer offers no simple remedy for moral injury—only recognition. Recognition that the grief we carry is not weakness, but proof that we remain fundamentally human, still capable of discerning right from wrong, still attuned to the sacredness of life. Perhaps this understanding is the truest repayment of moral debt we can offer: to never deny the pain, to never hide from the grief, and to bear witness openly, turning moral injury into moral insight.

In giving voice to the wounds we carry, we honor those who can no longer speak, repay in some small measure the wrongs we've witnessed, and begin the journey home—not to who we once were, but toward who we can still become.

Chapter 6: Ringing Silence

The Inner Blast of Brain Trauma No One Can Hear

"He fell heavily to the ground, and his armor rattled about him. As a poppy droops its head to one side when weighed down by the shower of spring, even so did his head bow beneath the weight of his helmet."

— Homer, *The Iliad*, Book VIII, trans. Samuel Butler, 1898 (public domain)

Science of the Invisible Wound

The battlefield is saturated with invisible forces—shockwaves, overpressure, concussive blasts—that injure without leaving a mark. For many combat veterans, traumatic brain injury (TBI) is not a single devastating blow but the cumulative result of repeated exposure to explosions, gunfire, and high-pressure events. These injuries are often silent and insidious, manifesting with or without the obvious signs of concussion.

Medically, a traumatic brain injury is defined as a disruption in normal brain function caused by a blow, jolt, or penetrating injury to the head. TBIs range from mild to severe, with "mild" TBIs including concussions. According to the Centers for Disease Control and Prevention (CDC), symptoms of a concussion include headache, confusion, dizziness, nausea, sensitivity to light or noise, and memory issues. These may appear immediately or hours later. (CDC, 2022)

Recent research from the Department of Defense and the National Institutes of Health has shown that blast exposure—especially repeated low-level blasts from heavy machine guns, mortars, shoulder-fired rockets, or breaching charges—can cause TBI without a classic concussion.

These sub-concussive blasts can still result in long-term changes to white matter integrity, neuroinflammation, and damage to the brain's electrical signaling. (VA Office of Research & Development, 2022) The symptoms often mimic PTSD: irritability, emotional numbness, sleep problems, anxiety, and impaired memory. However, unlike PTSD, these issues are rooted in physical alterations to brain tissue and function.

Stress and trauma exacerbate these symptoms. Chronic hyperarousal, common in both TBI and PTSD, places sustained pressure on the nervous system and impairs the brain's ability to recover. Veterans with both PTSD and TBI often experience worsened cognitive function, prolonged tinnitus, increased dizziness, and a heightened startle reflex. (VA Brain Sciences Lab, 2021)

In my case, the ringing in my ears—constant and unrelenting— becomes deafening in times of stress. The military taught us to ignore pain, but the truth is that many of us have been walking around with brain injuries we never knew we had.

I didn't read those studies until years later. Back then, I only knew that something inside me had shifted.

Boom, boom, boom…

Earlier, I wrote about the beginning of Operation Steel Curtain and how we took fire from the local mosque after entering the city. Later that same day, I was knocked unconscious by an explosion. At the time, I was serving as the assistant team leader. Our point man was on his first combat deployment. He was capable, but he was concerned that his lack of combat experience might cause him to miss something. To boost his confidence, I told him I would walk point and he could walk behind me. After clearing it with our team leader, we began moving.

We had been going for a while—clearing buildings, moving upstairs to rooftops for overwatch, then back down and on to the next structure. At one point, I turned a corner and was walking down the street when I suddenly felt something was off. I looked back, and at the corner about thirty yards behind me, my teammates were peeking around, watching me. On the opposite corner, two engineers were also peeking around a wall. The engineers were easy to distinguish because they all wore dark goggles.

Engineers blow things up—and I knew immediately that I was in trouble. My eyes moved from the engineers to a gate across the street from me. In Iraq, every house has a five- or six-foot wall around the property, with a metal gate at the street. On that gate was a can of TNT with a burning time fuse. The gate was about ten yards away. I remember turning all the way around and taking a few steps back the way I had come—then the TNT detonated.

The blast slammed me into the wall. When I came to, I was on my knees, gripping the small edges of the bricks with my fingertips, as if holding on for dear life. My whole body was tense. Fine dust hung in the air, stinging my eyes, coating my mouth, clinging to the sweat on my exposed skin. It felt like being underwater—I could hear, but everything was distant, muffled, and overlaid with the high-pitched ringing that drowned out the world. The disorientation was so complete it felt like I wasn't fully conscious, like my body was moving before my mind had caught up.

I stood and walked back through the haze toward the corner where my team had taken cover. My legs were wobbly, and I felt like laughing and puking at the same time. When I cleared the dust cloud, I could see them looking at me in disbelief. When my team leader spoke to me, I couldn't understand what he was saying—the ringing in my head drowned everything out. I smiled at him and pointed to my ear while shaking my head. He smiled back at me and put his hand on my shoulder. I unintentionally shouted at him, "I will walk in the back!" He shouted back, "OK!" I realized he was teasing me, and I felt the embarrassment come to the surface. In a much softer voice I said, "I fucked up" as I looked down at the ground. He shook my shoulder and when I looked back up at him, he slapped me on .the back, as if to say I'm glad you're still here. Then I saw him speak to the others and we stepped off again with me trailing the team.

There was no time to dwell on it. The day just kept escalating.

Later, the engineers blew up the mosque we had taken fire from when entering the city. They had discovered that the basement was packed with weapons and ammunition, so they destroyed it in place. I don't know how many satchel charges they used, but it was excessive. We were four blocks away when they detonated the charge, and the shock wave blew out all the windows in the four-story house we were on the roof of.

The dome and entire roof of the mosque flew over a hundred feet into the air before crashing down in a pile of rubble. My ears were still ringing from earlier, and the explosion startled me even though our RTO had warned us it was coming.

My team leader was on the rooftop access structure with his sniper rifle. He took two shots and then yelled down at me. I was one level lower than he was, sitting with my back to the parapet. The M-107 .50 caliber rifle sat beside me. I grabbed the big rifle, stood and planted the bipod on top of the wall. He talked me onto a doorway where armed men had just slipped inside. There was only one way they could have gone, and I emptied the ten-round magazine as I moved the reticle down the wall. Boom, boom, boom…

The .50 slams into you and surrounds you with pressure waves because the muzzle brake directs the gas back and to the sides. You don't want to be beside it when it goes off. Even with ear pro, it hurts. My body was buzzing as I searched the building for movement.

That rooftop fight blurred into the rhythm of the operation. The mosque, the detonations, the rifle's recoil—each moment carried its own concussion, until it all became one continuous barrage. And while I wasn't knocked unconscious again, the weeks that followed delivered more blast waves than both of my previous deployments combined.

We dropped 500-pound GBUs every day. We breached every gate and door we encountered. We stood behind M1 Abrams tanks and used the field phone on the back to talk the gunner onto buildings and windows, which they would then engage with the main gun. When the main gun fired, dust lifted off the street and walls, then settled back in swirling sheets.

We did all of this in confined spaces—inside buildings or on narrow streets with walls on both sides. In the breacher course, we had learned that shock waves bounce off walls and can compound in force, making explosives much more dangerous in urban environments than in open areas.

Echoes in the Body

What I remember most were the vibrations—the way they traveled up through the ground and into our bodies. Each weapon had its own signature: the low growl of an Abrams rolling down the street, the shriek of an AK-47, the thud of a 155 buried in the road, the teeth-rattling concussion of a 500-pound bomb, the world-stopping thump of a 1,000-pounder. Even the air changed shape as Cobra gunships dove low and fast or fighter jets screamed overhead.

When the operation was in full swing—Marines on both sides of the river, over 2,000 of us moving online and destroying everything that presented a threat—the vibrations never stopped. They moved through us as much as around us, leaving our teeth buzzing, our bones aching, our nerves humming.

The Ringing That Followed Me Home

During that operation, my ears never stopped ringing—and to a varying degree, they have been ringing ever since. There were no medical personnel coming around to the Marines to document our blast injuries for later care. No one cared, we just kept going.

The ringing never stops. It's like a high-pitched whistle buried in my skull—sometimes faint, sometimes piercing, but always there. Most days I can push it to the background, like white noise I've learned to live with. But when I'm tired, stressed, or in a quiet room, it's all I can hear. And it's not just sound—it's a kind of mental interference, a fog that creeps in and makes it hard to focus or respond.

My ex used to say something, and I'd catch only part of it. I'd have to ask her to repeat herself—sometimes more than once. At first, she was patient. But over time, it wore on her. She thought I wasn't listening. That I didn't care. And I couldn't blame her, because from her side, it must have felt like I was checked out. What she didn't see was that the noise in my head made it hard to even process what she was saying, let alone come up with a thoughtful response. I wasn't ignoring her—I just couldn't think.

Fog, Forgetting, and Fracture

It isn't just with one person, though. Noisy restaurants and crowded public spaces are some of the hardest places for me to be. The layered conversations, clattering dishes, music, and background noise all blur together until I can't track anything. It's not just that I struggle to hear—it's that I can't focus. The more noise there is, the more disoriented I become, until all I want is to escape to somewhere quiet. People across from me rarely got my full attention, not because I don't care, but because I'm overwhelmed.

I got some hearing aids from the VA and when I remember to wear them, they make a big difference in the noisy social scenes. They help me to differentiate between conversation and background noise. I wish I had gotten them a long time ago. A lot of dates would have gone better.

The same fog that makes it hard to follow a conversation also makes me forget things. I carry notebooks and write everything down now, building to-do lists so I don't lose track. I have forgotten enough important dates and things I was supposed to get done to know that I need help.

Sometimes vertigo hits without warning—the walls feel like they're closing in, and I have to take a knee and ride it out. If I listen to my body and get down, the dizziness clears in a few moments. If I don't, I risk blacking out and hitting the ground face-first.

It's impossible for me to know which of my symptoms are directly caused by traumatic brain injury. I've never had a single clean diagnosis—no MRI that lit up, no neat report that told me exactly what was wrong and what to expect. All I have are the changes I've noticed in myself over time. What I have noticed is that with a high stress load my symptoms get worse.

There's a particular kind of suffering in not knowing what's wrong with you. When you break a bone, there's an X-ray. When you get shot, there's blood. But when your mind starts to slip, when your emotions twist into something unrecognizable, when you can't track a conversation or finish a thought, there's no visible wound. No roadmap.

The injury tends to make a man isolate himself. When he's reminded again and again that he's being forgetful, that he's distant, when the people he loves grow frustrated with his condition, it makes him want to retreat. To stop burdening them. To be alone. But the silence and the loneliness become their own problem. Without someone to talk to—without a partner in life to reflect who he is—he can start to question his own sanity. In the quiet, the mind can turn against itself.

The gnawing uncertainty that something inside you has changed, and you can't prove it. That uncertainty corrodes your confidence. It makes you second-guess what's real and what's imagined. Am I just tired? Just stressed? Or is this the part where I start to disappear?

For Marines, uncertainty is weakness. You're supposed to know your weapon, your squad, your surroundings—yourself. But when the damage is inside your skull, hidden in the folds of your own brain, all that certainty unravels. And the worst part is, the world keeps moving like nothing's wrong. You look fine. You sound fine—until the moment you don't. Until you freeze mid-sentence. Or forget a promise. Or snap at someone you love and don't know why. The pain isn't just in the injury. It's in the silence that surrounds it.

Years of research now confirm what so many veterans like me have lived through: repeated exposure to blast waves—especially in urban combat environments—can alter the brain in ways that are profound, invisible, and lasting.

Naming What Was Hidden

A 2022 VA study published in the *Journal of the International Neuropsychological Society* found that veterans exposed to blasts within ten meters showed significantly worse memory performance, even in the absence of classic concussion symptoms like loss of consciousness (VA Office of Research & Development, 2022). This tracks exactly with what I've experienced—those moments where I forget a conversation from earlier in the day or find myself in a fog, struggling to hold onto a thread of thought.

The mechanism helps explain it.

Blast exposure can cause what's called "primary blast injury," where the overpressure wave from an explosion directly affects the brain without any external impact. These waves can disrupt the blood-brain barrier, cause inflammation, and damage neural pathways responsible for processing emotion, memory, and executive function. As the *VA Research Currents* notes, even veterans who were never knocked unconscious have reported ongoing issues with cognition, sleep, and emotional regulation after blast exposure (VA Research Currents, 2022).

My own internal conflict—the sense that I'm scanning for danger, looking for someone to blame, constantly preparing for confrontation—may also have a physiological explanation. Researchers have documented changes in brain structure following blast-related mild traumatic brain injury (mTBI), particularly in areas like the amygdala and prefrontal cortex that are responsible for emotion and impulse control. One study noted that veterans with both PTSD and TBI showed increased amygdala activity, impaired attention, and difficulty with emotional regulation (VA Brain Sciences Lab, 2021).

Even more striking is the evidence that blast exposure itself—
separate from any formal diagnosis of PTSD or TBI—has
measurable effects on mental health. A 2022 summary from the
Department of Veterans Affairs explained that veterans with high
levels of blast exposure scored significantly higher on tests for
depression, anxiety, and cognitive fatigue—even when no head injury
was reported at the time of exposure (VA.gov, 2022).

The longer I lived with these symptoms, the more I questioned
whether I was just losing my mind. But this body of research
confirms: no, I wasn't imagining it. The confusion, the volatility, the
sense that my mind was slipping—all of it can be traced back to the
concussive forces I endured day after day, month after month. The
shockwaves that blew through doors, into alleyways, and through
walls didn't just knock me unconscious once—they reverberated
through my nervous system in ways that are still unfolding years later.

In recent years, the Department of Defense and VA have launched
multi-million-dollar efforts to study these chronic effects under
programs like the Chronic Effects of Neurotrauma Consortium
(CENC). (Department of Veterans Affairs, 2022) New technologies
are being tested to monitor breachers and combat engineers in real
time, hoping to catch signs of neurological damage early, before
symptoms worsen.

But for many of us, that help came too late. We walked around with
ringing ears, scrambled thoughts, and buried rage, never thinking to
call it an injury. We blamed ourselves. We were told to tough it out.
And so we did—until relationships failed, jobs slipped through our
fingers, or our own minds became the battlefield.

But it doesn't have to be that way for those coming up behind us.
The research is there. The science is catching up. What's missing is
the cultural shift—the willingness to recognize that you don't need to
be bleeding to be wounded. That a man forgetting where he put his

keys might be carrying a war inside his head. That a short temper isn't always just attitude—it might be trauma echoing through damaged neural pathways.

If we can name it, we can fight it. We owe that to ourselves and to every young Marine still walking into explosions without understanding what they steal. The mission now is to speak. To be seen. To push for systems that acknowledge the silent casualties of war—and to make sure no one else has to wait until their life starts falling apart to realize they were injured long ago.

The Helmet That Fell Empty

When Homer described that empty helmet falling, he captured something timeless about war: its cruel invisibility, its capacity to inflict damage that cannot always be seen. On the battlefield, we recognize injuries through helmets pierced, armor shattered, bodies broken. But what about the warrior whose helmet remains intact while the defender beneath it suffers unseen wounds? Homer's image of a helmet crashing down empty speaks directly to the invisible devastation of traumatic brain injuries—the hidden wounds left by explosions that never leave a visible mark, yet hollow us from within.

In my own story, the ringing silence after each blast was my helmet hitting the earth—a signal that something inside me had changed, that a defender had fallen, even if no blood flowed. Repeated blast waves didn't just knock me unconscious or disorient me temporarily; they slowly rewrote the neural pathways of my brain. My symptoms—memory lapses, emotional storms, relentless tinnitus— were all warnings of a defender no longer fully present. And yet, because these injuries were invisible, I moved through life as if nothing had changed, dragging the shadow of trauma behind me.

The true tragedy of TBI is this invisible erosion, the quiet unmooring of self. For Homer, the fallen helmet was an emblem of lost potential, a warrior no longer able to defend himself or his comrades. For veterans today, traumatic brain injuries leave us similarly exposed, struggling silently beneath a mask of normalcy. The ringing in my ears that drowned out my loved ones' voices was more than physical—it was emotional isolation, a barrier I couldn't explain. The frustration and shame I felt when I couldn't understand a simple conversation weren't signs of weakness, but evidence of damage hidden deep inside my skull, damage no one could see but everyone around me felt.

Modern science now confirms what Homer intuitively knew: that war injures beyond the surface, that trauma echoes deep within us, reshaping how we experience the world. Research into blast-induced TBI reveals the profound yet subtle ways our brains can be altered without obvious concussion, transforming us silently and permanently. These hidden wounds aren't just medical problems— they are existential ones, threatening our identities, our relationships, our very sense of self.

And yet, there is hope in naming the invisible, in recognizing that silent injuries are real, measurable, and deserving of care. By speaking openly about these wounds—by refusing to let helmets fall without recognition—we transform suffering into advocacy. Our stories, our struggles, can become the catalysts for change, compelling military and medical communities to finally acknowledge what warriors have known since Homer's time: that some injuries never bleed, yet wound deeper than any blade.

By accepting that truth, I've begun reclaiming my life—not by denying my injuries, but by integrating them. I protect my hearing now, steering clear of loud environments when I can. I carry a notebook everywhere—not just to track what I need to do, but to capture passing thoughts about life, reminders of who I am. Writing helps anchor me when my mind drifts.

I meditate, exercise, and practice deliberate breathing to calm my nervous system. I've learned that when my stress level climbs— especially when I feel powerless—the symptoms multiply. So I work to lower the load. I train my body to stay strong, because physical exertion clears the fog in ways nothing else can. And I practice compassion toward myself. When I struggle to hear or forget something important, I try not to meet it with shame. I remind myself it's not weakness—it's injury. Eliminating negative self-talk has become as vital as any workout. Stress reduction and exercise are the most effective tools I've found to blunt the damage these injuries left behind.

My helmet may never have physically crashed to the ground, but the defender beneath it was nonetheless deeply hurt. The ringing silence is still there, but it no longer controls me. It reminds me that the most profound wounds are often unseen, and that true courage lies not in hiding those wounds but in openly confronting them.

Like poppies that bow yet endure beneath the weight of spring rain, veterans carrying silent wounds must recognize their resilience. Our scars may remain invisible, but our strength in facing them openly becomes an undeniable testament. Homer's empty helmet was not just a symbol of loss—it was also a call to bear witness, to recognize the quiet suffering, and to refuse to let any warrior endure it alone.

Part III: Reintegration or Isolation
Navigating Work, Identity, and Belonging After Combat

"Nevertheless, I long each day to reach my home and see the dawn of my return. And if some god wrecks me on the wine-dark deep, I will endure it."

— Homer, *The Odyssey*, Book V, public domain translation (adapted)

Chapter 7: The Compass Buried Within

Losing and Rebuilding Identity in the Wake of War

"I am Odysseus, son of Laertes, known among men for every kind of craft, my fame reaching to the heavens."

— Homer, *The Odyssey*, Book IX, public domain translation (adapted)

The Drift Begins

Existential drift is an unmooring that follows when the roles that once defined us vanish. This chapter shows that drift: a Marine returning home to no mission, a father watching his sons slip away, and a wanderer searching for meaning beneath the rain and sea mist.

Carl Jung described this kind of psychic unmooring as a breakdown in the ego's ability to orient itself in the world—a loss of connection between the inner self and the social roles that once gave it shape. In *Modern Man in Search of a Soul*, he wrote, "When goals vanish, meaning vanishes, and life becomes directionless. The individual drifts, unaware that the compass he needs is buried within." (Jung, 1933/1955)

That was me—adrift, and unaware of my internal compass.

When I left the Marines, I thought I was coming home to something—my two sons. I imagined reunion. I imagined becoming the father I hadn't been able to be while I was overseas. But by the time I returned, we were no longer the people we used to be.

My oldest son, ever the extrovert, adapted relatively quickly to my presence, showing me what he could do and telling me about his experiences while I was away. In contrast, my youngest son was more reserved and took longer to warm up to me. Even after we passed the initial awkward phase of our reunion, I faced a harsher truth: my boys seemed less interested in spending quality time with me.

They wanted to ride their bikes, play video games, and hang out with their friends. I understood—of course I did. They were just being kids, living their lives. But I had pictured something different. I thought we'd spend more time together, that I'd somehow make up for the years I'd missed. It wasn't their fault. It still hurt. I made the most of what I got and soaked it up whenever they let me in.

I drifted from one job to another. My brother initially helped me out by getting me some carpentry work, but the housing market collapsed in 2007, and new construction came to a screeching halt. I found myself living in a tent next to a buddy's trailer deep in the woods, taking on a job as a gunsmith to scrape by—a life of mere survival rather than one filled with joy and fulfillment.

I enrolled in the community college and signed up for classes during the day while working nights as a bouncer at a club that hosted hip hop and death metal shows. The hip hop crowds were generous with their tips, whereas the death metal fans weren't. One unforgettable night, chaos erupted when a massive woman in the pit swung at me. I ducked her wild haymaker and managed to get her in a rear hold to escort her out. Her boyfriend then snap kicked me in the gut, I grabbed him by the throat and drove them both into the wall.

That set off a full-scale riot. Around fifty people still inside turned violent—fighting staff, smashing furniture, breaking bottles. One of the bouncers grabbed an aluminum baseball bat, and we fought our way to the door. They shattered the front window just before the cops showed up. The next morning, I woke up with deep scratches across my back, no tips in my pocket, and a weak paycheck. I quit.

Seeking a better paycheck, I accepted a job as a bouncer at a strip club. The pay was decidedly better there, as dancers typically tipped the entire staff before their shifts ended. Often, by the end of the weekend, I would walk away with a thousand dollars in rolled up ones.

That fall, my sons played peewee football, and I made it a point to attend every game, capturing every moment with my camera. I cherished each experience, relishing the cheers from the sidelines, feeling as if I could finally be part of their lives. But then their mother's family moved back East—six states away—and she expressed a desire to relocate as well.

When the time came to give legal permission for the boys to join her, it broke my heart, but I signed the papers. They left after the football season, and when they did, it felt as if the ground had fallen out from under me, leaving me grappling with the void that their absence created in my life.

In truth, I was circling a drain. I was hanging around shady characters, and the longer I worked late nights in the strip club, the further I felt myself sliding into darkness. On nights I wasn't working, I wandered the city. I didn't have a dog at this time in my life—no anchor, no reason to go home.

One night I left a pub after a drink and found myself walking the railroad tracks. Walking had always been therapeutic, but this was different. I had drifted into the dark section where the homeless and the destitute gather. A flickering neon sign from a boarded-up liquor store threw pale light across the rails where I stood, but only a few yards away the shadows pressed hard against the walls—thick and black as the bottom of a well.

From beneath an old defunct loading ramp, someone started cursing at me. I couldn't see anything—just those inky black shapes—but the voice sounded possessed, like it was choking on the words as it spat them out. I stood there in the neon glow, motionless, watching the blackness for movement. Part of me wanted confrontation, but I couldn't step toward that vile, broken sound.

Eventually, I turned and walked away, feeling the presence burning on my back as I left. And as I walked, I knew: if I stayed in that world—if I kept living the way I was—in a few years I would be unrecognizable.

The Pacific Slowdown

So, I turned the bed of my truck into a makeshift sleeper and set off. North. Into the rain and grey of the Pacific Northwest.

With no plan, I survived on my savings eating dry goods—crackers, canned peaches, sardines. It was winter in the Pacific Northwest, and it rained almost every day. I spent long hours in the cab of my truck reading novels, losing myself in other people's stories. When the rain would break, I'd set out on the trails in Olympic National Park.

I followed the coastline south, climbing around on steep coastal cliffs to explore secluded tide pools. I poked at anemones, let hermit crabs crawl over my fingers, watched the surf roll in and napped in the sand. Every night, the rain returned. Once a week I'd find a laundromat. Every few weeks I'd splurge on a motel room and shave, shower, and remember briefly what it felt like to be human again.

When the skies cleared just enough, I set up my tripod and chased long exposures. I'd crouch on slick rocks as the tide receded, bracing against the cold wind, timing each shot between sets of waves. I would wait—ten, twenty, thirty seconds—watching the world blur while I stood perfectly still. Those photographs caught things my eyes never could: mist turning to silk, waves dissolving into glass, time itself stretched thin and luminous. I still have some of those photos. They remind me that even in my darkest drift, I was still reaching for the light.

One evening at a bar in Oregon, eating a bowl of clam chowder alone, a cowgirl sent her tough-as-nails father over to invite me to join them. After dinner she and I walked and talked for a while. I told her about the wars, about coming home and leaving again. She said she had a couple of kids and invited me to visit their ranch. I told her I would, but the next morning I headed south instead of inland. She was beautiful, and I knew even as we talked that I wouldn't stay. That night, climbing into the back of my little truck and pulling the blankets over me, I felt the sharp shame of not knowing who I was or where I was going.

In this solitude, I dropped to 185—survival weight. What mattered was that walking kept me human. Hiking kept me grounded and sane, while the isolation provided the space necessary to think deeply.

And that's what I did, step by step, mile after mile: I pondered fatherhood and the pain of failure, reflecting on my experiences in war and what lay ahead. I wrestled with questions, grappling with what my purpose was now that my boys were gone.

The longer I stayed in solitude, the more I noticed something remarkable: my stress levels dropped. Not all at once—but gradually, like mist lifting from the forest floor. My thinking grew sharper. Reason returned. Reading comprehension, once dulled by stress and fatigue, came back online. Creativity reemerged in quiet bursts— images, memories, and story fragments arriving unannounced as I hiked beneath the trees.

My body, too, began to ease. Even on a diet of canned fruit and dry goods, I felt better than I had in years. The constant ache in my joints subsided. My breath came easier. Long walks and hours of quiet movement—crouching, climbing, setting up shots—acted like a kind of physical therapy. I wasn't training for war. I was moving in harmony with the land. And that movement was healing.

I stretched without thinking—reaching, rotating, loosening hips and shoulders tight from years of tension. Movements came instinctively, not from a training plan, but from need. There was no finish line. No stopwatch. No yelling instructor. Just the rhythm of my breath, the crunch of trail underfoot, the slow pulse of the wilderness. It was restorative. Sacred. Mine.

I wasn't just healing—I was remembering. Not everything I'd lost, but everything I might still become.

Brotherhood Lost

One day, while wandering the serene expanse of the redwoods in Northern California, an old friend called me. He asked where I was and what I was doing, and I shared that I was living out of my truck. He mentioned he would be passing through San Francisco soon to visit family and invited me to meet up.

Accepting the invitation, I traveled south and camped out near the iconic Golden Gate Bridge, spending my days reading books and watching the waves roll in. When he arrived, we spent a few days together, and I was struck by how much I missed the camaraderie and brotherhood that had defined my life in the Marines.

When he offered me his couch until I could get a job and a place in San Diego, I said yes.

In *Odysseus in America*, Dr. Jonathan Shay describes what happens to soldiers when the bonds that once held them together—mission, brotherhood, responsibility—disappear.

Shay refers to it as a "collapse of character," not because the veteran lacks character, but because the narrative thread of who they are has snapped.

Dr. Shay often returns to Homer's *Odyssey* because it's the oldest story we have of a warrior trying to return—not just geographically, but spiritually. Odysseus doesn't just want to get home; he wants to become recognizable to himself again. That's the journey. And it's one modern veterans still face. (Shay, 2002)

We go from hyper-structured environments to chaotic civilian landscapes. From having a mission every day to having none. From being someone to being invisible.

And in that invisibility, many of us vanish—even while we're still breathing.

I am Odysseus, son of Laertes… known to the world for every kind of craft.

When Odysseus says this, he doesn't speak of home or peace or love. He speaks of skill. Survival. The ability to navigate chaos, escape monsters, build boats from wreckage. He's not bragging—he's naming the thing that's kept him alive.

I relate to that. I didn't come back from war with peace in my hands. I came back with *craft*. I could make things work. I could carry weight. I could build a life out of nothing, scrape by, disappear when I needed to, reappear when I had to. I could be whatever the moment demanded.

But I couldn't be still.

After the war, after my sons left, after the jobs and the drifting and the rain, I wasn't lost in one direction—I was lost in *every* direction. I wasn't searching for a place. I was searching for *recognition*. A version of myself I could live with. A story I could return to.

That's what *The Odyssey* is really about. Not the voyage, but the return. Not just getting home, but *becoming someone worth coming home as.* Odysseus doesn't just show up and get a parade. He walks back into his house as a stranger. He tests. He hides. He waits. Only when he's finally seen—*truly seen*—does the story begin to close.

But I wasn't close to home. Not in the way Odysseus was. I didn't even know I was looking for home. I wasn't searching for peace or rest. I was searching for something to be—somewhere to belong. An identity I could be proud of.

I didn't ask myself who I wanted to become. I asked the world what it needed me to be. I wasn't looking inward for direction—I was scanning the horizon for roles to fill. Marine. Father. Ghost. Whatever kept me from vanishing completely.

The truth is, I wasn't returning from war. I was still in it—just fighting on different ground. And when I looked around at the wreckage of my life, I didn't think, *How do I heal?* I thought, *Where can I matter?* And the answer, again, was the machine.

The first job I found in San Diego was cleaning boat hulls and doing underwater maintenance on boats in the harbor. It was a disgusting job. The harbor reeked of sewage, with liquor bottles and cigarette butts bobbing in the oily foam around the hulls. I had to wear two wetsuits, a farmer john and a spring suit, to stay warm while spending eight to ten hours a day in the water and I had to wash those wetsuits and my body with witch hazel every night so that I wouldn't break out with acne.

The Return to the Machine

On my breaks, I sat on the piers and watched helicopters flying into
NAS North Island. I told myself I should just go back to the
Marines—so I did. A few weeks of paperwork and I was in uniform
again.

This time was different. My orders sent me to 1st Force Recon,
which was being rebranded as 1st Marine Special Operations. I went
through the very first selection course and finished with strong
scores, but I wasn't chosen. Around camp I overheard instructors
talking about *Generation Kill*, the book Evan Wright had written after
riding with us during the invasion.

It had embarrassed senior leaders, and when HBO turned it into a
miniseries the resentment only hardened. My name was linked to that
story, and it marked me as a liability. No matter how well I
performed, the stain stuck. After a year of training with the unit,
command cut me orders back to 1st Recon.

At the same time, the battalion doctor forced me into surgery on my
right clavicle. An injury that was a few years old. I'd carried a pack
for hundreds of miles and finished Scout Sniper school and
MARSOC shooting packages with the separated clavicle, but he
refused to sign my jump school paperwork unless I agreed to the
knife.

I should have known I was in trouble the moment I met the
surgeon—gray slicked hair, plaid shirt under his lab coat, jeans and
Crocs. He looked more like a hungover carpenter than someone I'd
trust with my shoulder. He wasn't even Navy; he was a contractor,
paid to cut and teach the residents.

When I came to from the surgical anesthesia there was a nurse that
was begging me to stop cursing at her. I was angry but I didn't know

why. I know that I wasn't conscious during surgery, but I think in some way I was aware that they were hurting me badly. They cut the end of my clavicle off and forced a rubber strap over the top of the clavicle and screwed the other end to my scapula. The next day my shoulder and my arm were swollen and bruised.

Nine weeks later when I got out of the sling, I immediately developed a hematoma on my shoulder. The Navy surgeon had left a sharp edge on the bone when the cut was made. The moving of the shoulder caused the sharp end of the clavicle to cut through the rubber strap and begin cutting its way out of my shoulder. Lucky for me I was in Bridgeport CA when I had come back on limited duty and had to go to the doctor. I received my second surgery at a high-end clinic in Lake Tahoe and while the surgeon did an excellent job of repairing the damage the navy had done, he warned me not to screw it up again or no one would be able to fix it.

A few months later I was ordered into another MEU platoon that was beginning workup. I had to either carry a recon ruck on a fresh surgery, my second one in 6 months, or I could face medical separation. I wanted a career in the Corps so badly I chose to carry the pack—and it broke me.

I couldn't quit. It hurt so fucking bad, but the Marines was all I had to look forward to. I told myself that a miracle would happen, that sooner or later I would catch a break. The truth is, I didn't even know what I was doing—I just kept going. I didn't know how to quit. I didn't know how to ask for help. I was using whiskey and Motrin to get through patrols. I should have stopped and said I can't do this—that's what I would have done if I had loved myself.

I did damage that took over a decade just to begin healing. A recon ruck on insert can weigh between 80 and 120 pounds depending on what they are required to carry. It's ridiculous weight.

I was carrying that weight while trying to avoid further injuring my right shoulder. I would offset the pack to my left side to take the load off the right side. I kept reporting the pain to my platoon sergeant and to my corpsman, both of whom never reported it up the chain of command.

Breaking Point

Two months into the deployment while training in the jungle in Indonesia I was crossing a large fallen tree when I felt a popping in my neck and there was intense pain down my arm into my hand. The next morning when I woke up, I had lost the feeling in my right hand and arm. I didn't have any strength.

I couldn't pick my pack up. The command was confused that I was even allowed on deployment with the recent surgery, but they wouldn't send me home. So, I sat on the boat, because that's all we did on that deployment. We were at sea for three months straight while the air wing flew missions into Yemen.

After a few weeks I tried to do some exercise, hangs and push-ups, and I caused the injury to worsen and to migrate to my left side as well. At that point I was in terrible pain and eating muscle relaxers like they were sour patch kids. I slept in a coffin rack 18–20 hours a day. When we finally ported and put ashore in Dubai I was in terrible pain but happy to be walking around.

There were moments on that deployment when the pain was so intense, and the betrayal so raw, that I would shake with rage. My platoon sergeant had my orders changed, to keep me on the roster— knowing I was broken, knowing I should have been sent home. I trusted that someone in the chain of command would look out for me. No one did.

Every time I strapped on that ruck, I knew it might be the last time I could. And still, I kept going. Not because I believed in the mission, but because I couldn't stomach the idea of being forced out. I didn't want to quit. I didn't want to be discarded.

But deep down, I knew the truth—I couldn't stay in the Marines. Not like this. I would never carry those packs again. My body couldn't handle it, and my soul was already slipping away from the machine.

When I returned stateside, I got orders to the pool. My last eight months in uniform were a strange purgatory. No more field ops. No more rucks. Just morning formation, sunshine, and night classes. I was getting a tan and learning about wind turbines and solar panels— half Marine, half civilian already.

A few weeks before my EAS, I pushed myself too hard in a long swim workout—an hour in the pool, trying to prove to myself that I still had something left. When I got out, the pain hit me like a lightning bolt. I went to the aid station, desperate for relief, and was sent to the naval hospital for an MRI.

The results weren't surprising, but they were devastating: two herniated discs in my neck, two more in my lower back, and severe spinal stenosis—like plaque buildup inside the spaces around the vertebrae. My spine was closing in on itself.

They recommended surgery. A complicated one. But after what the Navy surgeons had already done to my shoulder, there was no way I was letting them near my spinal cord. I politely declined—and silently knew it was over.

So I took my honorable discharge and walked away from the Corps again. Not in triumph. Not with closure. But with a broken body and a quietly burning question: *What now?*

I had chosen to study renewable energy because it was more than a career path—it was a lifeline. I wanted to learn how to build my own systems, off-grid and self-reliant. Solar panels, battery storage, well pumps, small wind generators. Not just to work in the field, but to eventually live off it.

I wasn't dreaming of a return to society—I was dreaming of escape from it. A cabin in the woods. A quiet place. Something real I could build with my own hands. A kind of peace no one could issue or revoke.

When I left the Corps for the second time, it wasn't with medals or a sendoff. It wasn't even with anger. It was with a kind of quiet erasure. I didn't crash out. I faded.

The Nobody Self

In Homer's *Odyssey*, there's a moment when Odysseus is trapped in a cave by the Cyclops—a towering monster who eats several of his men. Odysseus knows he can't overpower the beast, so he outsmarts him. He tells the Cyclops his name is Nobody.

Later, when Odysseus drives a sharpened stake into the monster's eye, the Cyclops screams in pain, calling for help. But when the other giants come running and ask who's hurting him, he roars, **"Nobody is hurting me!"**

And so, they leave him.

That's how Odysseus escapes: by making himself invisible. By becoming Nobody.

I understand that. During that time in my life—drifting, re-enlisting, breaking my body for a mission that no longer made sense—I wasn't trying to be seen. I wasn't claiming space. I was just trying to survive. I became what the moment needed: a Marine, a shadow, a workhorse. I carried the weight and kept my mouth shut. I didn't cry out. I didn't rage. I adapted. I disappeared.

Gabor Maté, in *When the Body Says No*, speaks of the self that forms in response to trauma—not a self-chosen, but one adapted for survival. "We lose ourselves," he writes, "not because we're weak, but because we had to become what others needed us to be." (Maté, 2003) That sentence stayed with me. It explained why I didn't know who I was anymore—only what I'd been trained to be.

When the monster screamed—when the pain got so loud it shook me to my bones—nobody answered. Because that's who I had become.

Nobody.

Chapter 8: The Taste of Forgetting
Disconnection, Camouflage, and the Drift from Purpose

"But whoso ate of the honey-sweet fruit of the lotus no longer wished to bring back word or to return, but there he chose to remain with the Lotus-eaters, ever feeding on the lotus, and forgetful of his homeward way."

— Homer, *The Odyssey*, Book IX, trans. A.T. Murray, 1919 (public domain)

Culture Shock

For combat veterans, leaving the military is not merely changing jobs; it's losing one's tribe, identity, and sense of purpose. The civilian world, which promises freedom, often becomes a form of exile, driving veterans to seek meaning, camouflage their true selves, or retreat once again toward war.

In the military—especially in combat arms—your place is clear. The chain of command defines authority, risk is shared, and identity is fused with purpose. There's an implicit contract: you do your job, and others will do theirs, because lives depend on it. In the civilian workforce, those rules tend to dissolve. Deadlines might be suggestions, accountability could be soft, and workplace relationships are laced with politics, ambiguity, and performative smiles. Veterans who keep their heads down and work hard often make enemies without realizing it—their drive can make others look bad.

Psychiatrist Jonathan Shay, in *Odysseus in America*, writes about how veterans often find themselves frustrated or withdrawn in office environments. After years of depending on teammates in life-or-death situations, they return to find coworkers who don't communicate clearly, don't pull their weight, or treat work like a social game. Shay notes that this mismatch breeds alienation on both sides: veterans see coworkers as unserious, while coworkers see the veteran as cold, intense, or rigid. Even when unspoken, this tension erodes connection and reinforces the veteran's sense that they no longer belong. (Shay, 2002)

And yet, few veterans speak of this publicly. The discomfort of being misunderstood doesn't feel like a justifiable complaint. After all, they made it home. They have a job. What's there to be upset about? But deep down, they know: what they miss isn't just the military—it's *tribe*. The shared hardship, the unspoken loyalty, the clarity of mission.

When I got back to Camp Pendleton after my last deployment, I knew two things: my relationship with my girlfriend was over, and I was getting out of the Marine Corps. Beyond that, I had no plan. Just a lingering ache in my chest and the sense that something vital was slipping through my fingers.

Man's Best Friend

I went to the Longboarder Café one morning out of habit. As I stepped outside into the California sun, salt in the air, a young man with Coolio-style dreads sat on the sidewalk. A blue-nosed pit bull rested beside him—calm, alert, muscular, and lean.

"Nice dog," I said.

"Want to buy him?" he asked.

"What's wrong with him?"

"Nothing. He's just too big to live on the street with me."

I handed him a hundred bucks without hesitation. I was about to step into the unknown, and I didn't want to go alone.

"What's his name?"

"Biggie."

I opened the tailgate. "Come on, Biggie."

He jumped in like we'd been partners for years.

The next morning, I took him to the Del Mar dog beach. As the tide rolled in, he tore through the surf—biting at the waves, flipping, digging, barking like a lunatic. I sat on the rocks and laughed. Really laughed. I laughed so hard I collapsed into myself and cried.

It had been so long since I felt something that pure.

We became inseparable. Evening runs, truck rides, quiet nights. Everything I owned fit in the back of my truck. It was the simplest life I'd ever lived. And for a little while, it worked.

When it came time to leave Pendleton, I tied **my** Marine Corps–issued boots together and tossed them over a power line by the base pool—a final salute. Then Biggie and I drove north, for home, whatever that meant now.

A few weeks later, back in my hometown, I was working as a carpenter when a friend called to say she'd found a female pit bull with the same coloring as Biggie—abandoned, left to starve, needing a home. I drove over. In the warm sun, she was shivering with fear, too scared to take a step on the leash, a shaking skeleton. I carried her to the truck. Biggie accepted her with a quick sniff and a wag; I named her **Harley**.

Within weeks she put on muscle. She was wildly athletic—she could leap to the top of a six-foot fence, balance on the rail, and drop to the other side. She had a knack for letting herself out, avoiding cars and people, then returning to sit on the porch like she'd punched a clock. At the river, Biggie swam against the current while Harley rolled stones in the shallows, and fetched driftwood until her jaw trembled. Watching them love being alive gave me reasons to be alive.

They were active for the sake of being active and they loved to go hard, to push their bodies until they were panting and exhausted. They didn't have any reason to do the things they did except for the pure joy of doing them. That showed me the importance of recognizing the present moment and taking joy in life.

Everywhere I went, one or both dogs came with me. Biggie was the most fiercely loyal dog I had ever known. At a beach party in **San Onofre,** a drunk Marine decided he wanted to wrestle. I warned him—bad idea with Biggie watching. He shot in for underhooks; I let it happen. He turned me, and we hit the sand with him on top. A heartbeat later he screamed: Biggie had him by the ankle, tugging him off me. I laughed and pulled them apart.

They didn't care about rank or résumé. They just needed me to show up. When everything else felt unmoored, Biggie and Harley kept me from drifting. They gave me responsibility that wasn't about war. Morning walks. Evening runs. Two sets of eyes depending on me kept me from floating away.

Camouflage

I landed a job at a nonprofit called Black Rock Solar. I worked as an energy auditor, helping tribal communities lower their bills through efficiency upgrades. It was progressive, green, clean—but it was also alien.

I shared an office with women who did yoga, drank herbal tea, and spoke feelings with a fluency I hadn't earned. I kept mine sealed. They didn't know about the wars; they didn't ask; I didn't offer. I had already learned that certain words—**Scout Sniper** among them— land badly in civilian rooms, carrying a shadow into spaces built for safety.

So, I wore the mask: polite, useful, invisible. In staff meetings I felt like a tiger in a cage—calm on the outside while inside, a low rumble rattled the bars.

Some mornings, after a night of bad dreams, I felt a surge of anxiety about going in—being around people who couldn't possibly understand how I felt. I knew that I would seem distant and upset and that I might get asked what was wrong and there was no way I was going to tell, so I would call in sick. After this happened a few times, I thought I'd better get help before I lose my job.

I began seeing a therapist at the Vet Center, a woman who taught me how to breathe and how to listen to my body. She gave me tools. But healing was a spiral, not a straight path. Some days I felt progress. Other days I felt like a fraud, but it didn't matter because every week I went and talked to her. It was a crucial piece of my routine, week by week, learning to live without chaos. I would analyze myself, write things in my notebook, and she was someone, the only one who I had to share my thoughts with.

At first, I didn't know what to expect from therapy. I sat in the same chair each week, arms crossed, legs planted, eyes scanning the walls for details I hadn't noticed before. I wasn't there to talk about feelings—I just wanted tools. Something practical. Something I could use when the weight pressed down.

She never pushed. She guided. One day, sensing the agitation simmering beneath my stillness, she offered something simple.

"Just try this," she said. "Inhale for four, hold for four, exhale for four, hold again."

It sounded too basic to matter. But I did it anyway.

The moment I began counting—quietly, inwardly—something shifted. It was subtle, but real. The rhythm of the breath interrupted the chaos. My thoughts, usually racing and fracturing in a dozen directions, were momentarily silenced. My body, which often felt like a coiled wire, began to soften.

I learned to pull breath deep into my chest and hold for a slow four-count, take a small top-up sip and hold again, then exhale and pause. Within a few cycles my energy shifted. I even set a smile—habit before feeling—and it usually stuck. I used both anywhere: in traffic, in crowded places, before meetings, or on a mountain trail.

Breath changed posture, and posture changed feeling. With lungs full and chest lifted, my heart felt high; shoulders back, neck strong. The energy of that position was nothing like the collapsed one—lungs near empty, shoulders rolled forward guarding the heart. Lifting my sternum toward the sky made me feel present and in control, alive in my body instead of braced for impact. It wasn't a cure, but it was a reliable way back to the present moment: count, fill, lift, release.

Over time, it became more than just a technique. It became a discipline—a signal to my nervous system that I was safe, here, now. That I wasn't trapped in the past or barreling toward some unknown disaster. I was breathing. I was alive. And I was learning, slowly, to be at peace with both.

Radical Invisibility

Burning Man was in the BRS orbit, so I went three times. It was sold as transformation and truth, but I still wore my uniform of silence.

One evening, while we were building an installation, an older guy overheard me explaining camouflage to a friend—movement, outline, shine, contrast.
"How do you know these things?" he asked.
"I was a Marine."
"I've known quite a few Marines," he said. "I wouldn't have guessed. Your camouflage is good."

I smiled. It was meant as a compliment.

Later, in my tent, it didn't feel like praise. It felt like proof that I'd disappeared—not just from others, from myself. At Burning Man of all places, where everyone performs radical visibility, I was busy blending in: masking the edges, quieting the outline, dulling the shine, matching the contrast. I liked it. I was even happy. But I knew what I was doing. I was aware of my shadow and I kept it leashed, denying it any expression outside my skin. Camouflage worked; it kept me safe.

I started dating again, but something inside me flinched at real intimacy. I remember one woman—kind, beautiful, open-hearted. She made me feel safe, and that terrified me. I pushed her away without understanding why.

However, that was the first time I stopped and asked myself: What am I afraid of? What do I think I deserve? But at that time, I had no idea how much my childhood wounds were driving my choice in intimate partners.

After two years at BRS, I was able to get a home loan. I bought a small place that had tall ceilings and I set up a rope and rings in the middle of the living space. In the years after leaving the Marines I had been doing my own physical therapy to stay mobile. I ran and hiked with the dogs and my condition had improved in the years since leaving the Corps. I had drastically improved my lower back and hips with yoga-style exercises, but the problems with my neck and shoulders were still there.

The rope and rings suspended from my ceiling weren't just exercise equipment—they were a metaphor for all the invisible wounds I carried. Each morning, as I strained through stretches and therapy, I fought an enemy that lived unseen beneath my skin. My shoulders and neck held memories, locked in rigid muscle, knots formed by stress I hadn't fully confronted. Every pull-up felt like wrestling ghosts; each stretch was an act of rebellion against a body shaped by war.

In those quiet hours of therapy, I began to see how these injuries reflected deeper wounds—hidden traumas, emotional scar tissue I'd ignored for too long. My hips and back improved, loosening slowly with therapeutic exercises, symbolizing my gradual willingness to face and let go of the past. Yet my shoulders resisted, stubbornly painful, a physical echo of my emotional armor. They carried the invisible weight of everything I d seen, everything I'd lost, everything I still couldn't release.

Physical therapy became more than a routine; it was symbolic healing, a daily negotiation between holding on and letting go. Every improvement wasn't merely physical—it was proof that even hidden injuries can slowly heal if we have the courage to acknowledge they're there.

A Small Family

About a year later, I met a woman. She was a single mom. She was a hippie chick from the Eastern Sierra. When I walked her to the parking lot after our first date, I saw her old Jeep Cherokee on mud tires, and I wanted to know more. She dodged my attempt at a kiss but invited me to dinner at her place.

It wasn't just the mud tires on the Jeep or her refusal of my awkward attempt at a kiss that caught my attention—it was something deeper, quieter, harder to name. Perhaps it was the coyness in her smile or the way her eyes held mine steadily, openly, in a way that made camouflage feel unnecessary.

A week later, I met her daughter, a bright-eyed, fiercely curious four-year-old whose mind moved at a pace that both astonished and humbled me. The first time she took my hand to lead me to her bookshelf, selecting her favorite stories and reading aloud to me, I felt a tremor deep in my chest. It wasn't fear; it was recognition, a feeling so unfamiliar it took days to name. This was trust and adoration—she trusted me, and I adored her.

The more I spent evenings with them—meals around a small, scuffed dining table, bedtime rituals that included elaborate stories, quiet weekends outdoors—the more I felt myself anchored, tethered to something real. My existence, previously dominated by vague uncertainty and constant vigilance, began to solidify into moments I could count on. These simple routines weren't mundane; they were revolutionary, filling gaps I hadn't even acknowledged existed.

For the first time since coming home, I wasn't just surviving—I was part of something. I be_onged. This new family, tender and unexpected, became the ground beneath my feet, the stable point around which I hoped the chaos of the past could finally settle.

After a few months, we moved in together.

Then the bottom dropped out. The state job I took after BRS was crushed by a political shift. Solar funding dried up. My position vanished. With the job gone, fear rushed back in. I had spent four years learning renewables, and now the whole field was crumbling.

I was terrified I'd lose the family I had just found. I started doing carpentry for a contractor I knew from Little League to pay the mortgage.

Then a call came from an old Marine buddy. There was work. Overseas. Big paycheck. All I had to do was pass selection and get a clearance. He wouldn't tell me who the client was, but he told me to watch the movie *13 Hours*. So, I sat down with my new girlfriend and watched the movie. I had heard about the attack in Benghazi in 2012, but I had been intentionally avoiding news of the wars.

She was terrified of the idea, and I was thrilled. I tried not to show my excitement and calmly explained the practicality of me going back to a war zone for a few high-paying trips. We could remodel the house, we put some savings away, and I could go to art school on my GI Bill when it was over. But I had to make it onto the team first. Vetting was tough and I needed to prepare.

I told myself it was just temporary. Just a few trips overseas. A way to stabilize the family, pay the bills, and build a future. But deep down, I knew I was being pulled by something older, deeper, and more dangerous than money. The rhythm of deployment—the training, the team, the mission—was familiar. It fit me in a way nothing else had since I left the Corps. It felt like a return to something I could trust.

Why We Return

In *Odysseus in America,* Shay writes that many veterans, struggling with alienation and the loss of structure after military service, turn to work in private security or military contracting—not because they are mercenaries by nature, but because they are looking for the conditions of trust, clarity, and shared risk they once knew. Shay's point is that what draws many veterans back isn't violence. It's the conditions of tribe—mutual trust, clear roles, and shared danger (Shay, 2002).

In the civilian world, many veterans find themselves disoriented—not just by culture shock, but by the absence of meaning. There's no clear mission, no urgency. In that vacuum, returning to war—especially in a professionalized form that offers high pay and the illusion of choice—can feel like the only way to feel real again.

But as Shay warns, the return to professional soldiering often prolongs the injuries rather than healing them. What feels like regaining control can instead reinforce the split between the self and the world. Veterans in this cycle are not just seeking employment; they are seeking themselves in places that once gave them purpose. And in doing so, they risk becoming stuck in the space between—a place where purpose is borrowed, connection is transactional, and healing is deferred.

In *The Odyssey*, the encounter with the Lotus-eaters is brief, but haunting. After years at sea and countless battles, Odysseus and his men land on a strange shore. The people they find there are not hostile. They offer no violence. Instead, they offer something more insidious—sweet lotus blossoms that cause those who eat them to forget everything: their past, their purpose, and their longing for home. "Whosoever tasted it wished to stay there with the Lotus-eaters, ever feeding on the lotus and forgetful of the homeward way." Seeing the danger, he drags his men back to the ships and binds them to the benches so they cannot drift into forgetting. (Homer, *Odyssey* IX, trans. A. T. Murray, 1919, public domain)

The Lotus-eaters weren't evil. They weren't monsters. That's what makes them dangerous. They were just... removed. Passive. Detached. They lived in a haze of pleasure and forgetting, where memory had no sharp edges and purpose no urgency.

For many combat veterans, civilian life can start to resemble that island. It looks peaceful from the outside, even desirable. But without a mission, without that sense of shared hardship and belonging, the peace begins to feel more like drift—soft, numb, and quietly eroding the identity forged through fire.

The danger isn't that we fall into violence again. It's that we fade. That we become spectators in our own lives. That the very survival we fought for comes at the cost of forgetting who we were when we believed in something.

The longer we stay in that state—numb, disconnected, camouflaged—the harder it becomes to remember where we came from, and why we ever fought to return.

And in that forgetting, something essential dies.

Back to the Boat

When the funding dried up and I lost my job, it felt like failure—but in hindsight, it was the moment I was pulled back to the boat. Like Odysseus dragging his men from the haze of lotus-induced forgetting, the layoff forced me to reckon with a hard truth: I had been drifting. I had slipped into the quiet, camouflaged comfort of civilian life—useful, polite, invisible—but I was slowly forgetting who I was.

The routines, the therapy, the dogs—even love—anchored me, but without a mission I still drifted. The call from my old teammate wasn't just about a paycheck—it was a summons back to a world I understood. It scared me, but it also stirred something awake.

The job loss didn't break me. It shook me. It reminded me that I still had trials ahead. That I wasn't done yet.

So, I began to train again. To prepare. To focus. The next challenge loomed ahead, uncertain and far from safe. But I was moving again—not floating. I had returned to the boat, lashed myself to the oars, and turned my eyes toward the horizon, knowing that whatever lay ahead, I would face it not as a ghost of who I had been, but as a man still in the fight to become whole.

Chapter 9: The Rhythm of War

Deployment Stress Through Departure, Distance, and Return

"But Odysseus sat upon the shore, shedding tears, tormenting his spirit with lamentation and sorrow, as he looked out over the barren sea, weeping ceaselessly for his homecoming. So he spent his nights, for he was compelled to sleep in the hollow cave."

— *The Odyssey*, Book V, trans. A.T. Murray, 1919 (public domain)

The Beat of War

To operate in a high-threat combat environment, a man must make peace with death. He learns to push fear aside and numb himself to everything but the mission. But that numbness doesn't vanish when the deployment ends—it follows him home.

This chapter is about the rhythm of war: the departure, the distance, and the return. Not just physical miles, but emotional separation— between a man and his family, his partner, his former self. It's about the strain that repeated deployments place on a soul, and the silent unraveling that happens when he stops being able to love, connect, or rest.

These are not just my stories. They're echoes from hundreds of others—combat veterans who returned with a body intact but a heart gone quiet. What follows is how that rhythm played out in my life, and how the beat of war nearly drowned out every other sound.

Before I take you into my story, I want to share what the research says—because what happened to me isn't rare. It's part of a larger pattern that plays out in the lives of men sent into war again and again, and then expected to live as if nothing happened.

What the Science Says

Modern operational tempo—brief resets between repeated deployments—keeps the nervous system in a chronic state of activation. Trauma researchers describe a "kindling" pattern: repeated exposure sensitizes the system, eroding emotional regulation and leaving lasting physiological and psychological effects (van der Kolk, 2014).

Clinical work with couples mirrors this. Monson and colleagues link untreated PTSD with emotional isolation and higher conflict/divorce rates (Monson et al., 2009). Joiner's interpersonal theory helps explain elevated suicide risk when burdensomeness and isolation converge (Joiner, 2005).

Shay writes in *Odysseus in America* that modern warriors aren't broken by single events, but by **prolonged betrayal, grief, and moral compromise**. He argues that the hardest part of war is the return—because reintegration into a world untouched by trauma often feels impossible.

What the science confirms is what many of us already know: that war doesn't just wound the body—it fractures the soul. And without time, support, or meaning, those fractures widen with every trip back.

But data only scratches the surface. To really understand this rhythm, you have to feel it in your bones. And for me, it started with a dream.

The Empty Homecoming

During the invasion of Iraq, we were issued doxycycline to prevent malaria. One of its side effects was vivid dreaming, and I felt it full force. Night after night, I dreamed I was driving alone in the dark, searching for a place I had never been. Eventually, I'd find the house. My family would be inside, but there was always a strange man there. The kids didn't want to talk to me. She would be cleaning, ignoring me. Everyone would.

I couldn't shake the feeling that the dreams meant something. We had no communication back then—no letters, no satellite phones, no internet. But I knew. Somehow, I knew she was with someone else.

When I finally got home, my bank account was empty. She wouldn't answer my calls. I found out she had used the power of attorney I gave her to put herself on the account. She drained it, opened multiple lines of credit, and disappeared. I couldn't even take leave until I got paid again.

What I came home to was exactly what I had been dreaming of for months: betrayal, distance, and silence. She was with another man, didn't want me to know where she lived, and wanted nothing to do with me being a father to my boys. When I reached out to her family, I was treated like a violent criminal. The story they had already written—the one about the dangerous, unstable veteran—was in full effect. I wasn't violent. I wasn't angry. I was just hurt. I missed my kids. I wanted to tell them I loved them. I wanted them to know I had been thinking about them the whole time I was gone.

But I had to face reality. I had been gone nearly two years, and I had changed. So had they. I often think about a phrase someone once told me: *"Perception is reality."* What they meant was that other people's perceptions of you—no matter how wrong—can become the reality you're forced to live in. In their eyes, I was a threat. And for a time, I started to see myself that way too.

I hired a lawyer and went back to Southern California. The divorce was finalized without me having to return in person. Years later, after the fear and anger settled, I'd reconnect with my sons. But in that moment, all I wanted was to go back to war. At least there, I understood the rules. At least there, I knew who I was.

That homecoming left a deeper scar than combat. It made me feel vulnerable in a way I hadn't experienced on the battlefield. I still saw myself as a harmless kid. But through their eyes—through the training, war, and all the changes—I looked like a monster. And that's how I began to see myself.

Dead Man Walking

One of the quiet transformations that happens to a man at war is this: he must accept his own death. Not as a hypothetical—but as a daily reality. If he doesn't, it will unnerve him. It may get him killed or it may get others killed. Fear is paralyzing in combat. A man who fears death will hesitate when fractions of a second can be the difference between winning and losing.

That mindset followed me through life. Years later in Afghanistan, I carried an M67 frag on my belt when I left the compound. It wasn't for a fight; it was for the moment after — if capture was certain and I couldn't shoot my way out. That was the private calculation I made with myself: deny them the win, take some with me if I could. I never told my wife. You can't explain that kind of math at a kitchen table.

On my second deployment as a marine, I had no fear of death. In fact, I wanted to die in combat but that didn't happen. When I returned home, I was no longer the same man. I had seen behind the curtain on the Fallujah deployment. I knew the wars weren't about freedom or protecting the innocent. They were for profit. Young Americans were dying so that defense contractors and politicians could get rich.

Everything that once gave me purpose was gone. I didn't feel like part of a family anymore. I didn't even believe in the goodness of the country I served. I saw a ruling class that used violence to maintain power, and a public that had been manipulated into believing it was noble.

There was no homecoming celebration for me after Fallujah. No banners. No embraces. Like so many others, I turned in my weapon, dropped my gear, and went drinking.

That night, after the bars had closed, drunk and drifting down the beach, I watched Marines strip naked and run into the ocean. We laughed, screamed, and swam in the dark surf. To me, it was an expression of pure relief. No weapons. No IEDs. No ambushes. Just the crash of waves and a moment of freedom—freedom to be vulnerable again, and to play like children without worry.

During the workup to my third deployment, I dated casually—but I couldn't be serious about anyone, because I couldn't be serious about life. I knew I was heading back to war. I had already made peace with the idea of dying, though I didn't fully grasp the emotional distance that kind of acceptance carved into me. I was a dead man walking— alive in body but hollowed out inside. I could laugh, flirt, hold someone's hand—but I couldn't let them get close. My heart was already buried under sandbags and steel.

Whenever the conversation turned toward the future—What happens after your deployment? Where is this going? — I had no answer. I couldn't see past the next mission. Life after war was a blank page I wasn't ready to write on.

I started to notice it in the eyes of the women I met. That moment when they realized I wasn't just a Marine — I was a war junkie. Their kindness unsettled me. Their pity felt like a mirror, and I didn't like what I saw. So, I did what I knew best: I disappeared into the training program. War was the only place that made sense.

When that third deployment ended, I came home two weeks before the rest of my unit. By the time they landed back in the States, I had already hung up the uniform and started the long drive home to try being a father again. I didn't know it at the time, but in four more years I would be deployed again.

Ambien and a Gun

During the workup to my fourth deployment, I had a girlfriend that I was serious enough about to live with. For a short time in my life, she made an apartment feel like a home. I knew that we would not make it through the deployment, she had already seen too much of my shadow. Years ago, I wrote a story about a night in our lives during that time. Here it is in a paraphrased form from the original.

The transmission of my little Toyota pickup whines as I reach the top of first gear.
Traffic on the 5 is the same every weekday at 5 p.m. I shift the truck into second gear and pick up speed until I'm going twenty miles an hour; then, five lanes worth of brake lights in front of me are glowing red again, and I'm slowing down and shifting back into first gear. This is the way it is. It's not quite a full stop, but it's close enough to drive you nuts.

I saw the Battalion doctor for sleep issues. He asked about stress. I mentioned the commute, money, and my failing relationship—but avoided talking about PTSD.

My commute is forty-five minutes to an hour both ways. I have to be on base for the morning workouts by a quarter to six daily. By four-thirty in the afternoon. I'm tired, and I have to get in the truck and drive home in rush hour traffic. I fall asleep at the wheel, which scares me, so I drink some caffeine. Then I tell him the caffeine keeps me up all night. By Thursday, I'd logged maybe eight hours of sleep all week.

The doctor probed gently. "Is anything else bothering you?"

I told him money was tight. My girlfriend was in school, gas had hit $4.50 a gallon, and I had child support and rent. He nodded. 'Money can be stressful.' Then, again: 'Anything else?' I knew what he was fishing for—PTSD—but I wasn't going to give him that.

I admitted my relationship was strained, that deployment was looming, and I wasn't sure we'd make it. Eventually, he gave me Ambien. I didn't take it every night—just three or four times a week. It worked, mostly.

I didn't need one that night. It was the weekend—I could stay up, drink a beer, and unwind. I hoped we'd go out and have fun. Things had been hard lately.

Even when I did sleep, the dreams came. Not dreams—alternate realities. I'd be in a firefight, clearing malfunctions from my rifle, the enemy getting closer each time. I'd wake up soaked in sweat, heart pounding. Sometimes I was talking to dead children—broken, limbless, full of questions I couldn't answer: "Why did you hurt us?" Sometimes I was hiding from enemies, waiting to be found. The dreams and the talking in my sleep usually sent her to the couch.

The 73 was clear. I drove fast. Our apartment was nestled near a wildlife preserve in Laguna Beach, eucalyptus trees all around. I dropped $3 in the toll booth. Just across the street—home.

Her car wasn't there, so I parked up the hill and left her the assigned space. Inside, I took off my boots, unbuttoned my uniform, and sank into the couch. The apartment felt like home—clean, decorated, hers. My books were neatly shelved. She'd made it a place I could settle in.

Something caught my eye on the bookshelf. Not a book—my Colt 1911, the backstrap upright like a spine between novels. I retrieved it. It was off safe. I cleared the chamber and found a live round in my palm. How did it get there?

I sat with the pistol and when I pressed the slide release and the empty chamber snapped closed, I started to remember.

Ambien the night before. Watching TV. She was irritated. I delayed going to bed. The swells hit—like the room was a ship at sea. I staggered, bumped into walls. She warned me: "If you don't stop this, I'm going to leave." I told her I didn't want to be there either.

In the bedroom, I saw the framed photo collage of Iraqi kids. Usually it reminded me of the good, but last night, it reminded me of the dead. The ones we killed.

I opened the closet. Retrieved the pistol. Loaded a round. Sat on the floor. "I don't want to be here either." I aimed at my heart.

She took the pistol from my hands. I hadn't even noticed her arrive. She handed me a phone. "Talk to your brother."

I heard his voice through the line. Slumped over to the floor. Saw her bare feet. Passed out.

I was focused on remembering when I heard her heels on the walkway. I liked that sound.

I looked at the pistol in my hand, heart sinking.

She opened the door. Saw me. "You found it… do you know what you did last night?"

I nodded. "Yeah. I've been thinking about it for the last half hour."

"Did you hide this in the bookcase?" I asked.

"I was hoping it would take you longer to find it."

"How did I get to bed?"

"You crawled up from the floor in the early morning."

I looked at her—beauty, fear, exhaustion. Some love left, but frayed. I said, "I'm sorry."

She watched me, silent. I think she wanted hope. I couldn't give it. I was deploying again.

Part of me loved her. Part of me knew I'd lose her. She didn't want to hear about demons, she wanted them gone.

Again I said, "I'm sorry." It felt hollow.

She gave me a look—resignation. She was going to give up on me. And I was going to let her.

That night became a turning point, though I didn't recognize it then. I had tiptoed to the edge—not in a firefight, not on patrol, but alone in a quiet apartment with soft lighting and framed memories. That moment showed me what war had really done: not just the nightmares or the distance, but the silence inside me. The numbness. I couldn't feel anything until it nearly killed me. She saved my life that night, not just by taking the pistol, but by seeing me when I couldn't see myself. And still—I let her slip away. Part of me thought she deserved better. Part of me knew I couldn't be reached.

When I came back from that fourth deployment, she picked me up, drove me to my truck, and told me she was seeing someone else. I appreciated the honesty. I also knew it was coming. It still hurt.

The next morning, outside the Longboarder, I met Biggie—the blue-nosed pit I wrote about earlier—and took him home. Life has a way of handing you a leash when you need one.

Front Sight Focus

About six years after my last Marine Corps deployment, I stood on a cold firing line in West Virginia, waiting to start another qualification — the first step on my path as a security contractor. I reached into my coat for a piece of hard candy and pulled out a folded piece of paper instead. My girlfriend's handwriting: "Front sight focus," a small heart, her name.

I was staring at it when the man next to me leaned over and read it. "That's a down-ass bitch," he said. I slid the note back into my inside pocket and focused on the targets in front of me. If I didn't pass this qualification — and the four weeks of qualifications that followed — I'd have to go home and tell her I didn't have a job. That terrified me.

When I started contracting, something in me shifted. I let go of the idea that I could heal myself and decided sacrifice — my sacrifice — was the only way forward. I told myself I was doing it for the family:

provide first; everything else later. But the more I kept my eye on that single front sight, the more the rest of my life blurred — the body that hurt, the mind going quiet, the people waiting outside the armor. What I called discipline was, piece by piece, neglect. And it was wounding more than just me.

What I didn't understand then was that self-neglect isn't noble. It's destructive. The longer I ignored what was happening to my body — the chronic pain, the numbness, the creeping weakness — the worse it got. But I pushed through. That's what I thought strength was.

My first trip to Kabul hit hard. The third night in-country, we took incoming—two volleys, three mortars each. The first hit while I was in the shower. No sirens, no alarms—just that gut-deep recognition. The sound was unmistakable. I hadn't heard it in over a decade, but my body remembered before my brain did. That low thump and crash, then the dull recognition in your gut. I knew what it was before the radio call came.

I barely had time to dry off and throw on pants before the second volley landed. I was crouched down, pulling on my boots to sprint to HQ. That run—shirt still damp, adrenaline burning off the edges of thought—felt like stepping back into a life I thought I'd left behind. There were no follow-up attacks. Just silence. And then the surreal calm of the HQ break room, fluorescent lights humming, someone's half-finished puzzle, Afghan news on TV. I sat in there staring at the TV not understanding a word of it. I was back in a war zone. And it didn't feel like a dream. It felt like remembering who I used to be.

We operated in two-man teams, accountable to no one unless we screwed up. There was no daily brief, no chain of command breathing down our necks. We planned and executed by talking to one other person. Every day we crossed out of the relative safety of the U.S. compound and into the chaos of the city. Just me, my partner, a radio, an M4, and a Glock 17. No turret. No convoy. No attention. It was a completely different and yet still extremely exhilarating.

Before my first training drive in the city, I was anxious. I was going to do something that I had thought I would never do. After the contractors were burned and hung from the bridge in Fallujah, I had thought that job was not something I would be comfortable with.

Thankfully, I had a good man watching over me—an old teammate from the Marines, now my mentor on this new battlefield. He didn't say much, he didn't have to. His calm rubbed off. His quiet confidence steadied my hands. Within two weeks, it felt natural. The rhythm of it. The watching. The waiting. The readiness. War, it turned out, had never really left me. It had just been sleeping.

Home, Rearranged

When I came home from that trip, they were both waiting for me at the airport—my two beautiful girls. The moment I saw them, all the noise in my head faded. Her eyes lit up when she spotted me, and the little one ran full speed into my arms like a heat-seeking missile. I bent down, scooped her up, and held them both close. That's what a homecoming is supposed to feel like. Not a formation on the tarmac or a handshake from a CO—this. Warmth. Smiles. The sense that you belong to someone again.

We loaded up the car and headed home, the conversation light, the city outside familiar but distant. When we pulled into the driveway, something shifted. I walked through the front door, into the main room—and stopped. Everything had changed.

The layout was different. New furniture. My heavy bag was gone, along with the rings I'd rigged from the ceiling. No trace of the man cave I'd once carved out. The room had been domesticated—

smoothed over, softened, made into something more curated, more comfortable, more… hers.

I didn't say a word.

I didn't tell her the rings were part of my shoulder and neck rehab, that I'd been using them to recover from years of strain and impact. I didn't ask about the recliner that vanished into the digital ether of Facebook Marketplace. I didn't complain that my version of "home" had been edited while I was away.

Because I was just happy to be back. I'd made it home alive, and they were there. That counted for more than any piece of furniture. But still, some part of me took note. Not resentment—just a quiet awareness that returning home doesn't mean everything waits for you. Sometimes, it changes in your absence. And when you walk back in, the space doesn't quite fit the same. You make peace with it. You call it love. You tell yourself this is the price of a softer life.

After we got married, certain patterns emerged—ones I didn't fully expect. Arguments became common, and sometimes I felt more like a child being scolded than a partner in an equal relationship. It wasn't just the content of the fights, but how they made me feel. Confrontation, especially when it came with anger or raised voices, would shut me down. My nervous system locked down. I couldn't process words. I couldn't think clearly. My brain would go into survival mode—fight, flight, or freeze—and more often than not, I froze. I retreated. Emotionally and sometimes physically, I hid.

In a combat environment, I could stay calm until the last possible moment. Then—and only then—I'd let the fear in. Not because I wanted to panic, but because I trusted the training. The drilled repetition. The cultivated instinct. I had drilled my equipment into muscle memory, and rehearsed emergency procedures until they were second nature. I knew that when the fear came, it wouldn't paralyze me—it would activate me. My mind and body had been forged for that moment.

But when I saw the anger on my wife's face—heard the sharpness in her voice, saw her frustration pour out through every gesture—it triggered the same fear. It threw me straight into survival mode. The problem was, I had no training for that battlefield. No standard operating procedure for an angry woman I loved. No instincts worth trusting.

I remember retreating—literally walking down the railroad tracks near our house, trying to calm down, trying to understand what had just happened. I couldn't figure out why I hadn't been able to deescalate it. Why I couldn't charm my way through, or make her laugh, or turn the energy into something light. In that moment, my brain froze. Creativity vanished. Humor disappeared. All I could access were fear and anger, like those were the only tools left in the box.

This pattern repeated itself over and over: a fight, a shutdown, a retreat. And every time it happened, it felt like I was failing—not just in communication, but as a husband, as a man, as a person. The more I failed to speak, the more I felt unheard. The more I felt unheard, the more I withdrew. It became a silent spiral.

And all the while, my body kept deteriorating. The pain got worse. The numbness spread. My hands would lose strength. But I kept going. I told myself I had no choice. That to stop would mean failure. That to admit something was wrong would mean I wasn't strong enough. So, I ignored it. I pushed through.

But at some point, pushing through becomes pushing *past*—past the signals your body is giving you, past the emotional red flags, past your own needs. I was slowly vanishing, and I didn't know how to stop it.

By the time I reached my seventh deployment as a contractor, I had already been through the full gauntlet—shootouts at the front gate, car chases through city streets, suicide bombers vaporizing themselves and everyone around them, angry mobs swarming our vehicles, volleys of indirect fire in the middle of the night, and IEDs buried in the side of the road. I carried all of it in silence. I didn't talk to my wife about any of it.

Not the fear. Not the adrenaline. Not the moments that left me shaken or sick or strangely proud. I kept it locked down, buried under layers of practiced detachment. At home, I was quiet, distracted—still mentally sorting through images and sounds from Afghanistan while pretending to be present in a room full of people who had no idea what was echoing in my head. I think she read that silence as disinterest. Coldness. Like I just didn't care.

And yet, they were always there at the airport—every time I came back. Smiling, arms open, the little one smiling at me and reaching for her hug. For the first couple of weeks, it was always magic. The honeymoon phase. No arguments, no demands, just laughter, sex, dinners out, lazy mornings wrapped in blankets. We didn't talk about the next deployment. We didn't talk about anything hard. We just pretended we had all the time in the world.

Then came what I used to call the "honey-do" phase. The shift was subtle—romance replaced by routine. I'd fall into a pattern of drinking beers and working on the house during the day. Remodel projects, repairs, landscaping, checking things off the list we'd made while I was gone. I wasn't working out. I wasn't meditating. I wasn't decompressing. I was just killing time until it was time to leave again.

The final few weeks always carried a different energy—heavier, more emotional. Every conversation had a subtext. Every disagreement, no matter how small, hinted at the larger truth: that I was leaving again. We'd both start reaching for something to hold onto—more affection, more sex, more plans for the future. Trying to convince ourselves that this time would be the last. Every time we promised each other: just one more.

On my last trip to Kabul, I stopped training Jiu-Jitsu with the guys. I didn't say it out loud, but I knew why. After an hour of rolling, I'd be wrecked for two days. My shoulders would lock up, my neck would spasm, and I'd struggle just to get my kit on over my head. The pain was back in full effect, and it wasn't going away this time. I had made it through vetting. I had made it through seven deployments. I had made it through more fights than I could count. But my body had reached its limit. Quietly, it was giving up.

Changed People

I didn't know how to talk about that kind of defeat. I'd built a life around being the guy who could always push through. Pain wasn't weakness—it was familiar. But this felt different. It wasn't just pain anymore. It was breakdown. The joints that once gave me strength now betrayed me. The muscles that once made me proud now ached from the simplest movements. I was unraveling.

And I wasn't the same man she had met. Not even close. When we first got together, I was focused on healing—body and mind. I was studying energy, exploring Eastern philosophy, learning about electricity. Combat was in the past. Violence was something I had survived, not something I was still participating in. I was lean, thoughtful, curious. I was trying to become whole again.

But over the years—between the deployments and the distance, the arguments and the long silences—I had stopped. I stopped learning. I stopped growing. I stopped healing. The stress of the marriage, the constant rhythm of leaving and returning, had worn me down. My mind went quiet. My body followed. I let it all go.

She had changed too. The barefoot, crystals-and-sage hippie I'd fallen for had become someone else entirely—a born-again Christian with new convictions and a different language for everything. I no longer recognized her, not really. And yet, I was still willing to sacrifice myself for her. I told myself that love meant endurance. That if I just held on a little longer, it would all make sense. But deep down, I knew we were both hanging on to something that no longer existed.

When COVID shut down the world, it felt like permission to stop. Not just contracting—but everything. I didn't know who I was anymore. My body was failing. My spirit was numb. So, I enrolled in art school, and we endured the lockdowns and the masks and all the crazy propaganda.

I could feel the weight of the armor I no longer wore. Not on my shoulders—on my soul. Every argument, every silence, every time I couldn't find the words or the calm or the softness to meet her halfway, I knew what was happening. I hadn't laid down the sword. I had just learned to hide it better.

That's the strange curse of the warrior: you carry both love and destruction in the same body. You long for peace, but part of you only knows how to function in chaos. You want to be close, but you've trained yourself to create distance. And when you finally speak of home, it's already changed—or you have.

Now, years later, I understand that coming home isn't a single moment. It's a practice. A slow, aching, uneven return. Some men never make it. Some keep fighting even in kitchens and bedrooms. Some speak of love with swords still at their feet.

I've tried to lay mine down. Some days I succeed. Some days I don't.

But I keep trying.

Because somewhere in the rhythm of war, I started to remember what matters. And in the remembering, maybe I can find my way back—not to the man I was, but to the man I still hope to become.

Part IV: In Search of Home
The Journey Beyond Survival

"Then Penelope said to him, 'Stranger, I will go up to my room and lie down on that bed which I have watered with my tears so many nights, since the day when Odysseus went away with the sons of Atreus for Troy. But now you have come back to your own house, to your country, and to me."

— *The Odyssey*, Book XXIII, trans. Samuel Butler, 1898 (public domain)

Chapter 10: Down to the Bone

Rock Bottom, Recovery, and the Long Work of Healing

"But let me go my way over the barren sea, and suffer all, until I come to my home."

— *The Odyssey*, Book V, trans. A.T. Murray, 1919 (public domain)

Rock Bottom, Defined

Rock bottom is not merely the lowest point of suffering—it is a critical intersection where the destruction of old patterns becomes an opportunity for profound self-discovery and healing. This chapter explores how facing physical breakdown, emotional collapse, and personal loss creates space for recovery, resilience, and ultimately, a deeper understanding of oneself.

Rock bottom isn't a singular moment but a gradual, relentless erosion of self, leaving behind only the bare structure of who we once were. It strips away illusions, comfort, and false security, forcing us to confront truths we've long avoided. At this depth of pain, clarity emerges, and the difficult yet transformative journey toward healing can begin.

In my own experience, rock bottom appeared first as a relentless physical decline, mirroring the unseen emotional fractures deep within me. This profound deterioration became undeniable, marked by persistent pain, debilitating injuries, and a lifestyle caught in destructive cycles. But beneath the physical damage was a more devastating internal struggle—my choices, relationships, and self-neglect had compounded into a collapse so complete it left me isolated, exhausted, and hopeless.

It is here, at this point of total breakdown, that the possibility for real healing presents itself. True recovery requires more than mending the body; it demands a rigorous, honest examination of one's life, relationships, and emotional truths. The voyage back from rock bottom is solitary, arduous, and deeply personal, but it is precisely this journey that offers the promise of genuine transformation and lasting peace.

I learned this truth through raw experience, waking each morning with that piercing ringing in my ears—an incessant alarm signaling deep internal damage and too much stress. My cheeks were raw, flesh stripped away by relentless chewing in my sleep. When I looked in the mirror, I hardly recognized the man staring back. My face was hollowed and gaunt, my neck thin and tilted to one side, a painful reminder of my physical decline. My shoulders and neck ached constantly, a physical manifestation of the turmoil within.

Anger simmered just beneath the surface, a constant irritation I can't escape. An MRI confirms what I already feel: discs bulging severely into my spinal column, evidence that old injury has been made worse. I've been pushing myself through sixteen-hour days, and nights away from home, for over a year on a ranch in Texas Hill Country, working as a rifle instructor and hunting guide. A job I took on a whim to escape the feelings of inadequacy that came with spending my time drawing and making pictures during COVID. I am lost, trapped in an unfamiliar place, in a job that feels hostile, and within a marriage that is failing.

Physically, I am a shadow of myself. I can't manage a single pull-up or shoulder dip. Merely hanging from a bar sends sharp pain through muscles that have wasted away from disuse. My upper back and shoulders, my lats—all atrophied, visibly testifying to my decline. This land, which once promised freedom, now feels like a cage, oppressive and suffocating. All I want is to go home, back to the eastern Sierra and the mountains of the Great Basin, back to the only place that I ever felt truly free.

Reflecting on it now, my choice to move there—to sell my home and start anew—seems incomprehensible. At the time, I believed it was an opportunity to sacrifice for others. I lived to keep my wife and family happy, burying my desperate need for peace and healing beneath obligations and expectations. In doing so, I lost sight of myself, sacrificing my own well-being until nothing was left but exhaustion and regret.

The move that I'd framed as 'for us' had, in practice, erased me.

A Doctor's Question, A Friend's Counsel

Two doctors who reviewed my MRI report insisted surgery was the only path forward. Seeking a final opinion, I reached out to an old friend, my first platoon SARC (Special Amphibious Reconnaissance Corpsman), now a respected emergency-medicine physician at a prestigious university. When he examined my MRI, he confirmed the severity of the injury but advised against surgery. Instead, he shifted the conversation toward my lifestyle—asking about stress, alcohol, and sleep.

My answers revealed an unhealthy pattern: drinking three or four nights a week on the ranch, usually mixing beers and shots. Away from work, I relied on cannabis gummies to numb the persistent pain. My sleep was fragmented and restless, troubled by stress from a

hostile work environment and a strained marriage. Exercise had long
fallen by the wayside.

My friend spoke plainly: if I could change my lifestyle, I had a real
chance to heal without surgery.

But my personal life was unraveling. I wanted to leave Texas and
return home, while she insisted on staying. When our arguments
turned hostile, I packed my belongings and left. She hired a lawyer
and as soon as she signed the divorce, she shared pictures on her
Instagram—a new man, a new romance, a new family, a new life.
Though leaving was my decision to end the constant fighting, seeing
her move on so quickly inflicted a deep, heart-wrenching pain.

The images from her social media haunted me relentlessly, burned
into my memory. They were the first thing I saw in the morning and
the last thing I thought about at night. My emotions swung wildly
between guilt and rage, leaving me feeling as though I was losing my
grip on reality.

The psychic unmooring became an existential drift; betrayal stripped
the last names I knew—husband, father, warrior. In that slack water,
my mind started searching for any way to stop the pain and the
humiliation of being replaced.

For years my background had been a point of pride in our home.
When the marriage ended, the language around it shifted. "Recon
Marine" and "Scout Sniper" started reading less like a biography and
more like a caution sign. I'm not assigning blame—I have plenty to
own—but it's a pattern many veterans know: in conflict, the uniform
that once drew respect can be recast as a reason to fear.

Reaching for Help

Determined to find relief, one of my first actions was reaching out to my therapist to resume our sessions. She asked if I had heard about the Stellate Ganglion Block procedure or Ketamine therapy, explaining that some clinics combined both treatments with remarkable success. She sent me a video from *60 Minutes*, featuring a Green Beret who candidly shared his struggles with suicidal thoughts and the loss of friends to suicide. In the interview, after undergoing treatment, he was smiling and even laughing despite recounting painful memories. (CBS News, 2019)

Watching him, I knew instantly—that was what I wanted. Hope, relief, the chance to genuinely smile again.

I had been waiting for an appointment with VA mental health for three months. I went in for the intake appointment on the same day that I received the divorce papers to sign. The intake was exactly what I'd come to expect from the VA: detached, clinical, a stranger behind a desk asking questions from a script while typing my answers into a computer. But that day, the weight of it all pressed too hard. Somewhere in the middle of her long series of questions, I interrupted her. I can't even remember what I said—only that the words cracked open something inside me. I started crying, and I couldn't stop.

She waited in silence, her hands paused over the keyboard. No hand on my shoulder, no word of comfort—just the quiet hum of the fluorescent lights until I managed to get control of myself. Then she went right back to the checklist, finishing the questions as if nothing had happened.

My answers went into the system, and three months later I saw an actual psychiatrist. When the day came, I sat in his office and gave him my history—the deployments, the injuries, the divorce, the long stretch of sobriety I had fought to keep. I told him plainly: I didn't want to be on prescription drugs. I'm not drinking alcohol, I don't want narcotics, or antidepressants. I asked instead about alternatives—stellate ganglion block, ketamine therapy—anything that might treat the wound without dulling me into someone else.

He stood, walked over to a small whiteboard on his wall, and began to draw a brain. With the precision of a teacher, he explained how the medications would work on the different regions, describing neurotransmitters and chemical pathways in neat, rehearsed language. Then came the recommendation: Prozac, with Wellbutrin to counter possible side effects. If I stayed on the medication for a year and saw no improvement, he said, we could consider ketamine. As for the stellate ganglion block, he explained, they didn't perform that for psychological issues.

I didn't put up a fight or make an argument. I knew better. I walked out of the hospital without bothering to go to the pharmacy. They called me a week later and told me that I needed to come pick up my prescription. When I told them that I didn't want the drugs, they mailed them to me. I received a package in the mail that contained a full bottle of Wellbutrin and a full bottle of Prozac. I put them in the garbage. I don't want to disparage anyone from taking their medication but, I had used those drugs before and I knew that's not what I needed.

One day, lost in my own head, I drove straight through a red light. By luck alone, there were no cars coming. In that instant, I realized how far gone I was—that my mind was no longer under my control, and that years of trauma had hijacked not just my thoughts, but my entire body. I pulled the truck over and called a fellow Marine, a Purple Heart veteran and one of the best men I know. I didn't waste time with small talk.

"Do you know anyone doing stellate ganglion block or ketamine?" I asked.

"Yes, I do," he answered without hesitation.

The Protocol

That call led me to Dr. Shauna Springer at the Stella Treatment Center. After speaking with me on the phone, she recommended their SOF (Special Operations Forces) protocol. I scheduled my intake immediately, and a week later I was on a flight to Chicago to begin treatment at their main clinic.

What I didn't know then—but would later learn—is that this protocol wasn't experimental in the dark. Dr. Lipov and his team had already applied it to some of the toughest men on earth—Canadian Special Operations Forces—and published the results. In that cohort, combining four ketamine infusions with a Dual Sympathetic Reset produced an 87 percent reduction in neurobehavioral symptoms just two weeks after treatment (Lipov, Rolain, & Neufeld, 2025).

The SOF method was developed specifically to address the dual burden of post-traumatic stress and blast-related brain injury common among elite operators. By combining cervical sympathetic blockade—what Lipov later termed the Dual Sympathetic Reset— with subanesthetic ketamine infusions, the treatment aims to quiet the overactive fight-or-flight circuitry while simultaneously enhancing neural plasticity in the regions injured by trauma. In plain terms, one calms the storm, the other rebuilds the circuitry. For those living with bTBI, this pairing offers a rare route to relieve both the emotional and physical aftershocks of war.

Monday — First Infusion (and the First Laugh)

That first Monday morning, I was a mess of nerves. My hotel was only four miles from the clinic, but instead of getting a ride, I walked. It was winter in Chicago, so I laced up my hiking boots and layered a t-shirt, sweatshirt, and coat over my jeans. The cold air bit at me, but it wasn't enough to distract from the storm in my head. With every step, I replayed the spiral that had brought me there—the betrayals, the guilt, the anger, the shame. I couldn't shut it off. I knew balance had to exist somewhere in between, but no matter how hard I tried, I couldn't find it.

That morning, walking toward the clinic, I pinned my last shred of hope on the treatment ahead. Maybe, just maybe, it could help me find steady ground again.

My first session did exactly what I needed—it calmed me down enough to face the rest of the treatment. From the beginning, the staff went to great lengths to make me comfortable. A nurse started my IV, and once the doctor arrived, they layered me into a cocoon of calm: noise-canceling headphones over a sleep mask, pillows tucked beneath each arm, a blanket pulled across my chest.

It wasn't long before the drugs began to take hold. The calm gave way to paranoia, and I tore everything off except the IV and oxygen monitor. Sitting upright, I fixated on the color-changing lamp that painted the walls in shifting hues. That's when the nurse walked back in. She looked surprised to see me sitting there, wide-eyed.

"Can you feel it?" she asked.

"I think so," I said.

"Do you want more?"

I hesitated. "I don't know... do I?"

She slipped out, and a moment later the doctor entered and pulled a chair beside me.

"You alright?" he asked.

Leaning forward, still gripped by paranoia, I locked eyes with him. "Are you alright?"

He chuckled, leaned back, and adjusted the infusion pump before leaving the room. And then I left too—though in a different way. The next stretch was like being pulled through a wormhole of color, flying past strange, dreamlike destinations. I'd resurface in the room, recognize the shifting lamp light on the wall, and then vanish again into the current.

Eventually, I stayed. The beeping of the infusion pump told me the session was over. The nurse came in, shut off the machine, and removed the IV. "Just relax," she said.

But by the time she returned, I was already on my feet, dancing the last of the effects out of my system. She laughed. "I guess you don't need my help to walk." I laughed and then I followed her into the lobby, grabbed a few snacks, and waited for my ride back to the hotel. The whole thing had lasted about an hour, though it felt much, much longer.

It wasn't much, but I was laughing—and I hadn't felt a laugh in my own body in a long time.

On the way back to the hotel, reality returned—same memories, less bite—and I knew the next sessions would go better if I stopped fighting them.

I had a late lunch at a pho restaurant a short walk from my hotel. Then I went back and rolled out on my hotel room floor. After, I stared out the window at the flat Illinois skyline. I could feel the heaviness again. The weight of the loss and the aching in my heart. But my body felt better. During the time I was rolling out and doing my yoga on the floor, I could feel some tension release. It wasn't huge, but it was noticeable.

I fell asleep early, and slept well.

Tuesday — The River and the Reckoning

When I woke in the morning my shoulders and my body felt better than they had in a long time. As I was doing morning movement, the analogy that my shoulders had been struggling against a straitjacket and the ketamine had loosened the straps, came into my mind. That morning, I had a therapy session with the clinic psychologist before treatment to discuss the effects of the first infusion. I reported to her that my body was feeling the effects more than anything else, my neck and shoulders especially.

After our meeting I went back to my chair and the nurse started the IV. The second infusion pulled me under quickly. One moment I was in the clinic chair, the pump humming softly at my side, and the next I was swimming upward through a wide, slow-moving river. The water pressed cool against my body as my head slowly broke through the surface and I blinked the water from my eyes.

On the far bank, silhouetted against the pale horizon, I saw my ex-wife and her daughter. Their small hands were clasped in the grip of the man I had only seen in photographs. The three of them walked together, leaving the river behind. It felt as if, while I had been submerged, he had stepped in to take my place. The ache of that image cut deep, and I let myself roll onto my back, floating, staring up into an endless sky.

Then the current shifted, and I was carried elsewhere—not swimming but traveling, lifted through time. It was like moving with the ghost of Christmas past, slipping silently into scenes of every relationship I had ever been in. I hovered at the edges, not as a participant but as a witness, finally able to see what had always been hidden from me.

I saw myself in those moments—angry, withdrawn, defensive, numb. And I realized, with a sting of recognition, that much of what I was doing in the present was never truly about the person standing in front of me. My reactions weren't born in those moments. They were echoes—reverberations from betrayals long ago, from wounds I had buried and pretended were gone.

Every argument, every wall I threw up, every time I shut down—it wasn't about her, or the one before her, or the one before that. I was still fighting ghosts. Old pain was spilling forward into new love, and I didn't even know it.

The vision began to dissolve, the riverbank fading, the faces slipping back into shadow. I opened my eyes and the clinic came into focus again—the color-shifting lamp, the quiet walls, the faint hum of the machine beside me. A steady beeping cut through the silence. The infusion pump had run dry.

The nurse stepped in, calm and efficient, and silenced the alarm. She removed the IV with practiced ease and told me to relax. But this time there was no urge to jump up, no leftover energy pushing me to dance the chemicals out of my body. Instead, I sank deeper into the chair, heavy with what I had seen.

The day before, I had laughed and moved, letting the last of the drug spin through me like music. Today was different. I felt drained, stripped down, as if the infusion had wrung something out of me that movement couldn't shake loose. My body was calm, but my spirit carried the weight of recognition.

I wasn't eager to leave. I sat there quietly, letting the quiet settle over me, trying to hold onto the clarity that had come in flashes between the visions. When I finally stood to follow the nurse to the lobby, my steps were slower, my face still raw from the things I'd just witnessed. The snacks and waiting room chatter felt distant, almost unreal, as if I was still half in the river, half in the chair.

Afterward, I slipped back into the same routine as the day before. I walked to the little pho shop, ordered the same steaming bowl, and let the warmth settle me. Back at the hotel, I unrolled onto the floor, stretched, and stared out the seventh-floor window at the flat Illinois skyline.

But this time something was different. As I gazed out over the horizon, I felt a strange shift—like I was seeing myself clearly for the first time. Not just the man sitting there in that hotel room, but the whole line of him, traced back through the years. I followed that thread all the way to childhood, to the first cracks and wounds that had shaped me. The skyline blurred in front of me, and for a moment it felt like I was suspended between past and present, both clearer and heavier than before.

Wednesday — The Witness and the Boy

The next morning, I woke with an even greater sense of release. My shoulders, which had felt like they'd been bound in a straitjacket for years, were looser still, as if the straps had been tugged open another notch. The difference wasn't just physical—it carried a kind of quiet relief, a space inside my body I hadn't felt in a long time.

Before the next infusion, I met again with the clinic psychologist. I told her about the visions from the day before—about the river, my ex-wife, the man on the bank, and the ghost-like journey through my past relationships. I admitted how startling it had been to see the ways my old wounds had leaked into the present, shaping my reactions without me even knowing it. Then I spoke about the other side of it—the way my shoulders and neck had released some of their tension, like the body was letting go at the same time as the mind.

Not long after, I was back in the chair. The nurse started the IV and adjusted the monitor, and that was about it. No pillows, no blanket, no cocoon like the first day. I smiled to myself at the contrast— they'd gone all out to make me comfortable that first session, but by now I guess we all knew I didn't need tucking in. The hum of the pump started again, steady and soft, and I breathed in deep as the ketamine began its slow flood through my veins.

By the time the third infusion began, I had learned to surrender. The paranoia of that first day was gone, and the visions no longer startled me. As the medicine spread through me, I felt myself dissolve and then reform somewhere else—inside a stream of memories.

I wasn't living them. I wasn't even reliving them. I was *watching*.

At first, it was scenes with my two brothers when we were kids— fights, laughter, small cruelties that little boys inflict on each other without knowing why, swimming in the irrigation ditches and climbing the cottonwood trees. Then the scenes shifted forward: the Marine Corps, combat zones, nights out with other veterans, arguments with people I loved.

In every memory I saw myself as if through a pane of glass, no longer inside the skin of that man. From the outside, he looked young, confused, reckless, apathetic. I realized with a sharp ache in my chest that I felt sorry for him. He didn't understand why he acted the way he did. He was only reacting, doing the best he could with the pain he carried.

For the first time in my life, I felt empathy for myself. Not the kind of self-pity that spirals into anger, but something gentler—an acknowledgment that I was ignorant and naïve, but that I had meant well. That I had always carried the best of intentions, even when my actions were clumsy or destructive. That realization cut deeper than blame or regret: it was compassion.

Then a vision came like a gut punch.

I was in a courtroom. My friend sat at the defense table, his face ashen, waiting to be sentenced for murder. I remembered the real story: how he had acted in self-defense, how even the prosecution's own ballistic expert admitted it looked that way. But he had left the scene of the crime and the man he had shot was the son of a prominent figure in the community, and justice bent under the weight of influence.

Inside the vision, the weight of that injustice pressed down on me. I wasn't just watching—I was pulled inside the moment. I felt my body lurch, my eyes open, and suddenly I was back in the clinic chair. My voice tore out before I could stop it:

"Why did you shoot that man!?"

The question startled me and I looked up at the little red lights that indicated a camera. A moment later I sagged back into the chair, slipping beneath the current again, floating between conversations with men from my past, and clinic silence.

I surfaced like that several times, coming back into the room, talking out loud, only to drift away again. And each time I worried about what I was saying out loud, what conversations I might be having with the ghosts of those men. At one point, when the infusion ended, I asked the nurse if they recorded patients during treatment. She shook her head and said softly, "No."

A wave of relief and worry hit me all at once. Relief that my words wouldn't be preserved, worry about what I had just confessed. I knew I had been having conversations so real, so visceral, that I might have said things no one should hear. The boundaries between memory, dream, and testimony had blurred.

What lingered after the session wasn't the courtroom or the fear of what I'd said—it was the sadness for myself. The empathy. The recognition that I had been trying, always trying, even when my life looked like failure from the outside. That realization was as painful as it was liberating.

When I left the clinic that day, I carried less judgment. The man I had been wasn't my enemy. He was a boy carrying burdens far too heavy, doing the best he could with what he had.

Thursday — The Reset (Right Side)

Thursday was different. No ketamine, no colored lights shifting across the walls. Just the sterile brightness of the procedure room and the quiet hum of machines. That morning was for the first Dual Sympathetic Reset; a two-level block along the cervical sympathetic chain (often at mid- and lower-cervical levels) on the right side. I chose sedation so I wouldn't have to feel the long needle push into my neck or try to hold myself perfectly still.

The whole thing was over in less than fifteen minutes. When I came to, the nurse guided me off the operating table and into a chair. She asked how I felt. I paused, checked in with myself, and said, "I feel fine."

She smiled and asked if she should call my ride. "Yeah, sure," I said. She turned to go, and that's when it hit me.

A flood of emotion rose from nowhere. My chest felt tight, like a band was cinched directly across my sternum pressing into my heart. "Wait," I called out.

She came back quickly, just as I leaned back in the chair and lifted my sternum upward, pushing my shoulders back. A sudden release cracked through me—three loud pops in rapid succession, as if my ribcage itself was splitting open.

Her eyes went wide. "Was that your back!?"

"No," I said, almost disbelieving my own voice. "That was my sternum."

The words had barely left my mouth when tears broke free, streaming down both cheeks. I choked out, "What is this?"

She was already behind me, her hands on my shoulders, grounding me. "It's okay, sweetheart," she said softly. "It happens to all of you guys."

That simple truth undid me. I didn't even know what weight I had been carrying until it lifted. Something had unlatched around my neck, some old grip of tension I'd worn for so long it had become invisible.

That night, my dreams were filled with childhood—fights with my father I'd forgotten, the loneliness and the longing for affection, the pain of a boy who never felt safe in his own home. They weren't nightmares this time, not in the way I was used to. They felt more like a reckoning, the past surfacing and playing itself out without the usual painful emotions.

When I woke the next morning, a strange calm had settled in. It wasn't euphoria, but it was clarity. I realized my life was exactly what it was—not what I wished it had been, not what I feared it meant about me. Just what it was. And for the first time, I felt I could accept that story without guilt or shame. It was mine. All of it.

Friday — The Left Side and the Quiet

Friday began with the second stellate block, this time on the left side. I had learned something curious from the clinic staff: patients who respond most strongly to the left-side DSR almost always carry childhood trauma. I wondered what it would do for me.

The procedure itself was uneventful. No dramatic cracking, no sudden release like the day before. But when it was over, a profound calm settled into me. My body felt light, my mind unburdened. I couldn't put it into words at first, only that I felt a little bit like a child—unguarded, innocent, safe in a way I hadn't ever felt.

Before the last ketamine infusion, I met again with the clinic psychologist. I told her about the changes in my body—that the ketamine felt like it had loosened a straitjacket I'd been fighting against for years, and that the DSR had lifted what felt like a 25–pound weight from around my neck. I hadn't even realized how much pain I was living in until it began to recede.

She listened and nodded, but her words carried a caution. "If you return to a negative environment," she said, "these effects may not last. This treatment is only the beginning. The real work is what you do with it."

Her message struck me. Relief was possible, healing was possible—but it wasn't magic. The treatment had opened a door. What lay beyond was up to me.

Later that afternoon, I returned to the chair one final time. The nurse started the IV, the pump hummed, and I let go. This last journey was the simplest, the most blissful. I drifted through clouds and slipped into wormholes of shifting colors—violets, blues, and golds folding in on each other, opening into vast corridors of light. There were no courtrooms, no battles, no ghosts tugging at me. Just peace.

When the final infusion ended, the glow it left wasn't showy or ecstatic—it was quiet, contained, and resolute. For the first time in years, my body felt lighter, my mind steadier, my heart less encased. The treatments hadn't erased my history, but they had cracked open the possibility of living within it—not *in spite* of it, but *because* of it.

What remained wasn't a blank slate—but a space: for acceptance, for repair, for real work. I'd stepped off the edge of rock bottom, but the climb back wasn't over. The real voyage—hard and solitary—was just beginning. Yet now, for the first time in a long time, I could stand on that edge and say: "Let me finish my voyage—not with numbness, but with clarity. Whatever the danger."

Meaning-Makers

What I went through that week wasn't random. It wasn't magic. It was grounded in the work of two clinicians whose ideas gave purpose to what felt like a break—not a break from trauma, but a break open—when I needed it most.

Dr. Shauna "Doc" Springer was the first clinician I spoke with at Stella Treatment Center—and not by cold outreach, but because a Marine brother, a Purple Heart veteran I trust with my life, told me to call her. She took my call graciously and listened to my story—not clinically detached, but deeply human. Her book, *WARRIOR: How to Support Those Who Protect Us*, unpacks healing not as erasure but reintegration. It's about finding connection again, rebuilding trust in a world that can feel fundamentally broken. That first conversation with her didn't cure me, but it cracked the door open—it let me believe that this place might actually get me. (Springer, 2021)

Dr. Eugene Lipov, founder of Stella Treatment Center and inventor of the Dual Sympathetic Reset, comes at trauma from a different angle—but a complementary one. In *The Invisible Machine*, he argues that trauma isn't a character flaw or an endless psychological sentence—it's a physical injury to your body's autonomic nervous system (ANS). His DSR procedure, targeting the stellate ganglion with anesthetic, literally resets the stuck fight-or-flight response, which for many trauma survivors stays on high alert long after the danger has passed. (Lipov & Hallett, 2022)

What I experienced Thursday—cracks in my sternum, sudden tears, weight lifting from my neck—wasn't some metaphor. It was a physiological shift: my ANS resetting after years of strain. I didn't walk out cured; I walked out recalibrated—offering myself the chance to do the real work of healing. Ketamine helped me witness my story with empathy. DSR lifted the physical armor I'd worn so long. And the human guidance I received afterward—especially that insistence that healing would be built afterward—gave me the roadmap, not the finish line.

The Odyssey reminds us that every voyage worth taking carries danger, and every return demands courage. The quote I chose to open this chapter with—*"Let me finish my voyage—alone, whatever the danger"*—sang in my ears as I walked out of that clinic in Chicago.

I wasn't "cured." I wasn't free of the past. But I no longer had to carry it as a prison. The straitjacket had been shed. The weight around my neck was gone. And with a body unbound and a heart uncaged, I was ready to face the seas ahead.

It wasn't an escape from pain. It was the beginning of a true return: the choice to sail on, not in denial, but in clarity. To live with my wounds, not against them. To finish the voyage—whatever the danger.

I'd lashed myself to purpose for years; now I could finally row toward home.

Chapter 11: The Warrior in the Garden

When Vigilance Becomes Reverence

"Then Odysseus rejoiced in his heart, and straightway spoke among them, saying: 'Hold now, ye men of Ithaca, from grievous war, that so with all speed ye may part, and without bloodshed.'"

— Homer, *The Odyssey*, Book XXIV, trans. A.T. Murray, 1919 (public domain)

The Body Remembers

In summer I work the herb bed with a short-handled hoe, the same grip I would use on a weapon—stance squared, breath settled—breaking clods instead of bodies. I kneel into rosemary, thyme, and sage, pinching basil to keep it from bolting, checking leaf undersides for aphids the way I once checked doorframes for wires. The patrol line is a drip hose now; the only incursion is mint trying to go AWOL through the gravel. A hummingbird strafes the lavender, Stella noses the mullein and sneezes, offended. I chuckle. The hands that once cleared rooms now bruise leaves to release their oil and wipe loam on my jeans. Same vigilance—different vow.

Stress and emotional trauma do not vanish when the moment of danger passes—they inscribe themselves in the body, tightening muscles, hardening fascia, altering posture, disrupting breath, and even shaping long-term health. But just as trauma leaves its mark, deliberate practices—exercise, creativity, meditation, and connection with nature—can rewire the nervous system, restore balance, and help the body relearn its capacity for vitality and healing. Recovery is not about erasing the scars of war and pain, but about transforming how that energy moves through us, turning vigilance into awareness, discipline into care, and survival into life.

For years, I carried war in my shoulders, in the collapse of my chest, in the way my eyes never stopped scanning people's hands, waistlines, demeanors. The body keeps the score, and mine was written in tension, vigilance, and pain. But what I've learned—slowly, stubbornly, sometimes against my own instincts—is that the same body that bears trauma also carries the blueprint for healing. Stress imprints itself on us, but it can also be unwound, redirected, and transformed.

I've come to see that healing doesn't mean erasing what happened; it means teaching the body a new language. The vigilance that once searched for ambushes can be turned toward watching clouds move across mountains. The prayers I whispered in fear can become rhythms of peace, and the wild horse of my mind can be steadied with meditation, breath, and music. Even in the aftermath of war, nature offers a place to move, to breathe, to let energy flow again.

This chapter is about that transformation—how trauma takes root in the flesh, and how movement, meditation, and creation can help the body remember not only how to survive, but how to live.

A Map for What Hurts

I had learned to feel trauma in my body, but I didn't yet have a language for what was happening inside me. I knew my chest collapsed under stress, my shoulders locked up, my breath caught before it could fill me—but I didn't know how to explain it beyond "pain." Then I found Anodea Judith's *Eastern Body, Western Mind*. Her framework gave me a map for something I had always felt but never named. *(Judith, 2004)*

She describes the chakras not as mystical symbols, but as centers of energy that shape our development—each one linked to a different stage of life and a different part of the body. When trauma strikes in childhood, it doesn't just wound the mind or the heart; it interrupts the flow of energy that should move freely up and down the body.

Whether you read chakras as metaphor or as an energetic map, the model gave me a precise language for patterns my body had been acting out for years.

The first chakra, at the base of the spine, is about safety and belonging. If you grow up in chaos, it can leave you feeling rootless, always ready to move. The second chakra, in the pelvis, is about emotion and pleasure. Trauma there can shut down intimacy or leave you searching for comfort in self-destructive ways. The third chakra, in the gut, holds our willpower and sense of self-worth—when it's wounded, control and power struggles often take its place.

The fourth chakra, at the heart, is the bridge between the lower instincts of survival and the higher instincts of love. A closed heart chakra doesn't just mean you can't love well; it means you can't let love in. And then there's the throat, the fifth chakra—the center of truth, voice, and expression. When the throat is blocked, it's like a dam in the middle of a river. Energy can't flow up or down. The heart can't pour out love and compassion, and the wounds of the lower chakras can't move upward to be healed.

That's exactly what my therapist had sensed in my frozen scapulas. My voice had been locked down for years. I'd learned as a boy to silence myself, to hide what I felt, to keep my truth buried. That silence didn't just stay in my head—it lodged itself in my body. My throat became the gatekeeper of my pain, and in shutting it down, everything above and below it suffered.

I saw this most clearly in my marriage. My ex-wife's anger and frustration had the same weight, the same sharp edge, that I remembered from my mother. Whenever her voice rose, I froze. I hid my feelings because I was afraid that if I let them out, if I answered her anger with my own, I would lose my temper completely. I swallowed what I wanted to say, locked it down inside, and pretended it didn't matter. But the truth is, it did matter. Every silence built pressure. Every unspoken word added weight. Until finally it came out sideways—in bursts of rage, in slammed doors, in the kind of silence that cuts deeper than shouting.

Judith describes the symptoms of a blocked throat chakra as difficulty expressing yourself, feeling like you're not heard, or swinging between silence and explosive outbursts. That was me. I hid from my ex-wife's anger the same way I had hidden from my mother's. I thought silence would protect me, that burying my words would keep me safe. But all it did was trap me in the same old pattern: fear, silence, eruption, regret.

For the first time, I began to see that healing wasn't only about the mind, or even just about emotions—it was about energy. About finding my voice and letting it move through my body, so that my heart and my survival instincts were no longer at war with each other. Judith gave me a language for something my body had always known: until the throat opens, the rest of the system remains blocked.

And my body kept score. My neck would stiffen so badly I could barely turn my head, the muscles like braided steel cables pulling me down into myself. My shoulders stayed tight and raised, as if I were bracing for a blow that never came. My chest often felt locked, as if the simple act of taking a full breath was dangerous, like it might let all the words I was holding back come spilling out.

Opening the Gate

I began to see that my throat wasn't just about speech—it was the gateway for everything else. When it was closed, love couldn't move out of my heart, and pain couldn't move up from my gut to be healed. Energy stayed trapped, boiling inside, until it broke through in ways I couldn't control. Judith gave me a language for what my body had always known: a closed throat is like a closed life. Until the voice opens, nothing can flow.

For years, my silence felt like safety, but it was a prison. My voice was locked down, and with it, my body was locked down too. My neck, my shoulders, my chest—they carried the cost of every word I didn't speak.

The shift began with treatment. The dual sympathetic reset and the ketamine therapy were the first cracks in the dam. Those sessions didn't just quiet the storm in my nervous system; they opened space inside me that had been sealed off for decades. For the first time, I wasn't drowning in anger or frozen in silence. I could hear myself. I could feel myself.

That was the beginning of finding my authentic voice. Not the hardened voice of the Marine who barked orders, not the defensive silence of the boy hiding from his mother, not the strained calm of the husband trying not to explode—but a different voice. A voice that belonged to me. The shadow parts of myself—the anger, the grief, the shame—were still there, but instead of running from them or burying them, I began to speak from them. They weren't enemies anymore; they were part of my story.

Writing this book has been the continuation of that work. Every page has been an act of opening my throat, of saying aloud what I once believed had to be hidden. It has been my way of stepping into humility, telling the truth without armor, without pretense. Judith says the throat chakra is about authentic expression, about letting your truth resonate in the world. For me, that truth is this: I was wounded, I silenced myself, I carried that silence in my body for years—but I am learning to speak again.

Voice wants company, and mine finds it in the images and sculpture I create.

After years of feeling locked down, I returned to art school and put my work into the world again. My photography and drawings began to appear in shows, hanging on gallery walls where my community could see them and respond. To my surprise, people didn't just look—they recognized the work. They said the work carried weight, that it had something true in it. For a man who once carried silence like armor, that recognition felt like a kind of homecoming.

And it didn't stop with photography. I picked up my pencils again, returning to drawing after years of leaving that part of me behind. The pages began to fill with original works—raw, imperfect, but mine. Each line was another way of opening the throat, of letting expression move through the body instead of being trapped in it. Writing gave me voice, art gave me vision. Both were proof that creativity is more than pastime—it's medicine, a discipline of healing.

And as my voice has returned, the body has followed. My shoulders don't carry the same weight they once did. My chest opens more easily. Pain still lives in me, but it no longer defines me. My body is learning what my spirit is finally remembering: that expression is not weakness, it's freedom.

This book isn't just about war, trauma, or survival—it's about finding a voice after years of silence. It's about speaking in a way that is neither rage nor retreat, but something truer, something whole. And that voice, at last, feels like mine.

Cracks in the Dam

I had a vision that came to me like a map for living. Imagine standing in a high meadow, looking up at a tall mountain. From where you stand, you can see the trail leave the tree line and switchback upward until it disappears into the clouds that encase the peak. You know that is the way—the path toward purpose, toward the soul's higher calling. But there are other trails too. Lower trails that wind through the woods and along streams. They are easier, gentler, and they give the illusion of progress. But no matter how far you wander, those trails always circle back to the meadow, to the same place you started, looking up again at the mountain you were meant to climb.

The high road is different. It's steep, lonely, and long. It demands everything. But it also leads upward—beyond comfort, beyond repetition—toward the summit where the soul discovers its purpose. Each of us has to decide whether we will keep looping the lower trails or begin the climb.

Taking the high road wasn't just an idea—it showed up in my body. The first climb wasn't up granite switchbacks but through the tight armor of my own chest. For years, even the simple act of drawing a full breath came with pain.

Whenever I inhaled deeply, it felt as if my heart pressed against the frozen blade of my left scapula, like my chest couldn't expand without running out of room. Each breath was a reminder of what I couldn't say, what I couldn't release. My body carried the silence the same way it once carried armor—tight, unyielding, braced for a fight that never seemed to end.

I don't have that pain anymore. Somewhere along the line—through therapy, through ketamine and DSR, through learning to let my shadow speak instead of burying it—the dam in my chest broke open. Today when I breathe, the air moves freely, without the stab of old wounds. My heart no longer collides with my bones.

It feels, in a way, like returning home after a long exile. Not the home of my childhood, with its violence and silence, but the deeper home Odysseus longed for on his wanderings: the place where a man can finally lay down his weapons and speak in his own voice. My journey hasn't been toward comfort, but toward authenticity. To breathe freely, to write honestly, to live humbly—that is my Ithaca.

Homer wrote of men scarred by war, men who wandered for years carrying their grief in silence, searching for a way back to themselves. For me, that way back has been found in breath and in voice. What once felt frozen is moving again. What was locked has been opened. The silence that ruled my body is giving way to something new: a rhythm of truth, a cadence of healing, a voice that finally belongs to me.

But healing didn't stop with breath or voice. My body carried other habits too—the restless eyes, the scanning that never stopped. Even after my chest opened and my breath came freely, my gaze still swept every ridgeline, every horizon. The body remembers. But just as silence could be broken into voice, vigilance could be reshaped into awareness.

Warrior's Eyes, Garden's Gaze

These days I walk with Stella, my bird dog, every morning, usually five miles or more. The old habits of scanning never left me—my eyes still sweep the ridgelines, trace the horizon, notice the smallest flicker of movement. In Afghanistan, those same eyes locked onto different details: hands, waistlines, the twitch of a shoulder, the set of a jaw. I searched a man's eyes not to see him, but to calculate his intentions, to decide if he meant to kill me.

Now the scanning feels different. Out here in the high desert mountains, what I find isn't threat. It's rhythm. I watch the cycles of the wild things—the deer, the hawks, the insects humming low in the brush—and I try to see how their lives connect with mine, how all of us are woven into the same earth. Even the water has a rhythm. Clouds rise up heavy over one range, drop their weight as rain across another, then drift on, feeding the next valley. This is the Great Basin's way, passing life from mountain to mountain, an endless circuit of giving and receiving.

The mountains give me other reminders too: the sharp smell of sage after a storm, the throaty call of chukar roosters warning their covey, Stella pointing and creeping forward at the same time, her body quivering with instinct. I find shards of obsidian in the hills, black glass left behind by ancient forces, and I think about how long vigilance has been part of the human story.

I watch the wild horses running their own patrols across the land. I cast flies into mountain streams and alpine lakes, my awareness tuned not to ambush but to the flicker of trout beneath the surface. Even the warning rattle of a snake hidden in the rocks meets me differently these days. Once I would have killed it without hesitation. Now my answer is simple: live and let live.

There are nights when I hike up high and sit beside an alpine lake, watching the stars scatter themselves across its surface. Back then, I searched a man's eyes for danger. Now, I search my own intentions in the reflections of the constellations. Out here, vigilance has become reverence. I'm still fully aware of my surroundings, but the awareness is no longer chained to fear—it's an invitation to belong.

A part of it all—still a little disconnected, maybe, but a part nonetheless.

The same shift that changed how I used my eyes began to change how I used my body. Just as vigilance could be redirected from fear to reverence, movement could be transformed from punishment to care. Healing wasn't about abandoning the instincts the war had carved into me—it was about reshaping them into rhythms that kept me alive in a different way.

Movement as Care

The first time I managed a pull-up after treatment, I nearly cried. My body had wasted away so badly that even hanging from a bar once sent sharp pain through my shoulders, neck, and lats. Years of stress and neglect had left me hollow. In the Marines, exercise had always been punishment or preparation—pushing until something broke so you'd be ready for war. Back then, movement was about domination: dominating the body, dominating weakness, dominating the enemy.

But something shifted. Exercise became about care. Self-love.

I still train with weights, but the purpose is different. I've learned to listen to my body. Sometimes the old injuries insist on rest from the barbell, and when they do, I trade the iron for movement. Cardio and mobility take over: sprints, skipping, jumping rope, or dancing— always to music. People like to preach about discipline, about silence in training, but I don't buy it. Music is ancient. It's what our ancestors danced to around the fire, beating drums under the stars. It's what brings me alive, connecting body and spirit. For me, movement isn't only about strength—it's about rhythm.

My training now is high-intensity and playful. I'll run sprints, then skip, then dance, then walk, and then repeat. I let the music lead me through bursts of power and flow, my body remembering that movement doesn't have to hurt to mean something. And every day, I give attention to the places that carried the heaviest burden: my shoulders. With a simple wooden stick, I work slow arcs overhead and behind my back, retraining the scapulas and collarbones to move with symmetry instead of pain. In the doorway, I press my shoulder blades together, focusing not on force but on balance. I lean with my scapulas against the wall and gently push them flat. I am teaching my body a new language—one of patience, symmetry, and release.

Exercise is no longer about fighting. It is about repairing. It is about reminding my body that it is still mine, not just a weapon handed over to the service of war. Research confirms what I feel every day: exercise lowers cortisol, regulates the nervous system, and rewires the brain for resilience through neuroplasticity. But the science only proves what I already know in my bones—that strength, when it's chosen for care instead of combat, doesn't just keep me alive. It keeps me human.

Just as vigilance could be reshaped into reverence and exercise could shift from punishment to care, I've also had to relearn how to move through the chaos of my own mind. The body carries trauma, but so does thought. Without discipline, my mind would bolt the way it always had—into fear, into memory, into the past. Meditation became the next language of healing, a way to take hold of the reins.

Reins for the Mind

There's an old Buddhist story that captures the nature of the mind. A farmer was working in his field high in the hills. He looked down toward the city and saw a rider burst out of the gates, charging across the countryside on a galloping horse. The farmer watched as the man thundered through the villages, up into the hills, closer and closer. When the rider came near, the farmer stepped down to the road to see him pass. As the man flew by, the farmer called out, "Where are you going?" The rider shouted back, "I don't know—ask the horse!"

The horse is the mind. Left untended, it runs wild, dragging us into fear, memory, distraction, or despair. We think we're in control, but most of the time we're just hanging on. Meditation isn't about stopping the horse or breaking it—it's about taking the reins.

The first reins I ever held were the beads of the rosary. I've said hundreds of thousands—maybe millions—of Hail Mary's. In combat, I rolled the beads through my fingers in the quiet moments before hell broke loose. At other times, the prayers lived in the back of my mind while my hands worked like a tuned machine. Even now, my rosary hangs from the bedpost. Before sleep, or when I'm shaken awake by dreams, I pull it down and pray myself back into rest. The beads are a rhythm, a tether, a way of holding the reins when my mind wants to bolt.

My therapist introduced me to transcendental meditation, giving me a mantra in a small ceremony. At first, my mind fought against it— the horse bucking, pulling, bolting. But if I stayed with the mantra, returning again and again, something shifted. By ten minutes, the ride steadied. By twenty, I felt as though I were floating in ether, untethered yet calm. Not every attempt worked, but when it did, TM offered a clarity like sunlight breaking through fog.

Other times I used playful discipline. I'd count backward from one hundred, imagining each number painted in light across the dark of my eyelids, stretching the pause between numbers longer and longer until the horse bolted. Then I'd bring it back. If I lost my place, I started over. By the time I reached zero, my mind felt sharp and steady, as if the horse had finally fallen into rhythm.

And sometimes meditation wasn't stillness at all. Sometimes it was movement—jumping rope, sprinting, dancing to music. People talk about discipline as silence, but I've never believed that. Music is primal. Our ancestors danced around fires, playing music that spoke deeper than words. For me, movement to music is meditation—a looser set of reins, but reins all the same.

Meditation doesn't look only one way. Sometimes it's prayer beads. Sometimes it's a mantra. Sometimes it's numbers or music. But all of it is about the same thing: learning to hold the reins of the mind. To stop being dragged by the runaway horse and to ride with intention.

And sometimes—on the far side of practice—the horse stops altogether. The dust settles, the gallop slows, and something powerful emerges. Not silence in the ordinary sense, but a stillness with its own weight. Floating. Expanding. Dissolving. That moment when the horse finally stops is the doorway—to be conscious in the space of the unconscious.

Meditation gave me the same gift as hiking or training—it reminded me that I am not just a passenger of war or trauma. The mind can be steadied, the body can be retrained, and both can be reclaimed with practice. Breath, movement, vigilance, prayer—each is a way of teaching the nervous system that life doesn't have to be a battlefield. Together, they have become my disciplines of peace.

My shoulder blades are moving more every day. What was once frozen is loosening; what was once armored is relearning how to move with balance and symmetry. Strength and coordination are returning, but not in the way they once did. I'm not rebuilding a weapon. I'm retraining a body to live.

That is what healing looks like. It isn't erasure—there is no way to undo the years of tension, the restless eyes, the memories pressed into muscle and breath. The scars remain. But the body can be taught to carry them differently. Survival energy can be turned into creativity. Hypervigilance can become presence. Even pain can be reshaped into rhythm.

I see it in my shoulders, no longer clenched in silence but moving in symmetry. I see it in my vigilance, once hunting for danger, now searching for hawks, deer, and the constellations mirrored in alpine lakes. I feel it in music and movement, in the way scars turn into rhythm when I let my body dance, pray, or breathe. The old instincts haven't vanished—they've been redirected.

Healing is not about forgetting the war, or pretending the body hasn't been marked by it. Healing is about transformation. It is about turning what once kept me alive into what now allows me to live.

In *The Odyssey*, Athena commands Odysseus and the suitors' families to make peace at once and end this war of iron. For me, that line isn't just about Ithaca—it's about the body. The war of iron I carried in my shoulders, my breath, my vigilance, is beginning to end. The armor is loosening. The horse is steadied. The weapons are set down.

Athena's command has become my own practice: to make peace with my body, to let vigilance become reverence, and to allow survival to be transformed into life.

What felt experiential soon showed up in the literature.

What the Research Says

What I've lived in my shoulders, my breath, and my vigilance is not just metaphor—it's been studied and described by some of the leading voices in trauma and healing.

Bessel van der Kolk writes that trauma quite literally reshapes both body and brain. *(van der Kolk, 2014).* He points to how movement and exercise restore regulation to the nervous system by lowering cortisol, recalibrating the autonomic balance, and rebuilding the neural pathways that trauma erodes. Aerobic activity, weight training, and even playful movement stimulate neuroplasticity, encouraging growth in the hippocampus—the part of the brain responsible for memory and learning—and strengthening the prefrontal cortex, which governs decision-making and impulse control. When I hike or train now, I'm not just keeping my muscles alive; I'm reawakening parts of my brain that had been dimmed by years of stress and hypervigilance.

Meditation offers a different but equally profound transformation. Neuroscientists Richard Davidson and Antoine Lutz have shown through brain imaging studies that mindfulness and transcendental meditation don't just calm the mind in the moment—they change its architecture. *(Davidson & Lutz, 2008)* Their work demonstrates that consistent practice thickens cortical regions linked to compassion and emotional regulation while softening the grip of the amygdala, the alarm center that keeps trauma survivors locked in fear. What I experience when I sit with a mantra, when the wild horse of my mind finally falls into rhythm, is not just personal relief—it is the very neurological shift these researchers describe: the transition from a brain hijacked by survival to one capable of presence, compassion, and clarity.

Creativity, too, has its own body of evidence. Cathy Malchiodi, a pioneer in expressive arts therapy, shows how drawing, painting, music, dance, and writing help trauma survivors process experience without being overwhelmed by it. *(Malchiodi, 2007)* Art engages parts of the brain and nervous system that words can't always reach, offering safety where language has been weaponized or lost. For me, the act of writing this book has been just that—a practice of transforming silence into voice, and turning the scars carried in my body into rhythm and story. What feels like personal necessity is also what the research calls integration: the reweaving of body, memory, and meaning.

And then there is nature. Roger Ulrich's studies on stress recovery and Stephen Kaplan's work on attention restoration theory both describe the profound impact of natural environments on the human nervous system. Ulrich showed that even a few minutes of viewing natural scenes can lower blood pressure and muscle tension, while Kaplan explained how the "soft fascination" of landscapes—clouds moving, water flowing, leaves stirring in wind—gives the brain space to recover from overstimulation. *(Ulrich, 1991; Kaplan & Kaplan, 1989)* What I feel in the Great Basin, watching storms roll across ranges and wild horses cut their patrol lines across the valleys, is the lived expression of their findings. The land itself rewires the body. Where vigilance once locked me into threat detection, nature now invites me into belonging.

Together, these voices—van der Kolk, Davidson and Lutz, Malchiodi, Ulrich, Kaplan—confirm what my body already knows. Exercise, meditation, creativity, and nature are not luxuries; they are practices of survival transformed into life. They show that healing does not erase trauma but teaches the body, mind, and spirit to carry it differently—to turn vigilance into reverence, scars into rhythm, silence into voice.

Make Peace at Once

The last words Homer gives to Odysseus are not of conquest but of restraint: *"Hold now, men of Ithaca, from grievous war, and part without bloodshed."* For a man who had survived ten years of siege and another ten of wandering, the final act was not another battle, but a surrender to peace. That ending haunted me. If even Odysseus, hardened by iron and loss, had to lay down his sword, then maybe peace wasn't a grand treaty signed by nations—it was something smaller, more immediate.

Which was why *making peace at once* couldn't stay abstract for me—it had to live in a single evening, a single breath, a single choice to name what had been in the shadows and meet it without flinching.

I stood with Stella on a ridgeline as the light fell—range after range laid out in browns, purples, and blues. As the sun's last rays burned through the clouds, my shadow drew nearer: the boy who had reached for affection and found only cold rejection; the teenager who had no purpose and learned to sabotage himself; the veteran who had seen that the soul's wounds in war were ancient and unoriginal. I understood that denying those parts a voice had been making me sick.

Below us, the world kept humming—headlines refreshed, markets traded after hours, drones circled their orbits while citizens scrolled past war as if it were any other source of entertainment. Blood turned to balance sheets, outrage to algorithms; the machinery of profit wore the tone of patriotism.

On that slope I could imagine how a civilization ends: not with a single decision, but with a long refusal to face its collective shadow. Not left against right, but numbness against responsibility.
Stella pressed against my leg, nose testing the wind. I named the pieces of myself—boy, saboteur, survivor—and said, quietly enough that only the sage heard it, that they all belonged. The sky smoldered to ember. When we turned for home, the ranges were still there, unchanged, but the war inside had one less trench.

This is the work I mean by peace—to name what lives in me and in us, to speak it, to take responsibility for it, and to refuse the script the machine hands out. That moment opened the epilogue, where making peace meant owning the shadow.

Epilogue: Choosing Peace in a Wounded Culture, Reclaiming Our Humanity from the Ashes

War is a racket. It always has been. It is possibly the oldest, easily the most profitable, surely the most vicious… A racket is best described, I believe, as something that is not what it seems to the majority of people. Only a small inside group knows what it is about. It is conducted for the benefit of the very few, at the expense of the very many.

— Smedley D. Butler (Butler, 1935/2003)

Not Blame, But Clarity

This isn't an indictment. I said that in the beginning, and I need to say it again here at the end. I've written about my childhood, my parents, my marriages, the Marine Corps, and the wars. I've told truths that cut deep, but this book was never about blame. I don't blame my mother for the wounds she carried into her parenting. I don't blame my ex-wife for the pain we couldn't hold together. I don't even blame the Marine Corps, or America, for demanding too much from young men like me.

War is not only fought on battlefields; it is embedded in our culture—transmitted through trauma, sustained by hidden power structures, and disguised as normal life. If the young are to inherit more than ashes, they must learn to see these systems for what they are, refuse to serve them blindly, and choose to build something better. This is how we break the cycle: by naming the war we were born into and daring to end it.

Hurt people hurt people. As Gabor Maté writes, Trauma is not what happens to you, but what happens inside you as a result. (Maté,

2010)—and what festers inside us inevitably spills into others. None of us are raised in isolation; we are shaped by the wounds and coping strategies of those who came before us, and by a culture that prizes toughness over tenderness, production over connection, silence over honesty. My mother carried her wounds, I carried mine, and my ex carried hers. All of us were just trying to survive inside a culture that doesn't make it easy to raise children, to love well, or to live whole.

Survival has been rebranded as virtue. Most families now need two parents working forty, fifty, even sixty hours a week just to stand still. They spend their days trading time for money, and their nights trying to buy back scraps of time with what money is left. Their children grow up in the glow of screens while they chase paychecks that never catch up. And if they stop running, even for a moment, the ground vanishes beneath them. There is no door out—only exhaustion on one side and collapse on the other.

The Machine Has a Human Face

We call it normal life, but it behaves like a machine. It takes your hours, your body, your relationships, and feeds them into an endless grind that never remembers your name. It will burn anything—love, time, bodies—if it keeps the lights on. But it is not a machine. It is people. People who breathe and bleed, just like you, who chose power and greed over love and duty.

People who built a world that rewards extraction over care and then convinced the rest of us that this was freedom. We are taught to admire their success, to chase their approval, to measure our worth by how well we serve their systems.

Trauma doesn't just wound individuals—it becomes culture. As Bessel van der Kolk has shown, trauma reshapes the brain and nervous system, creating patterns of hypervigilance, emotional numbness, and disconnection (van der Kolk, 2014). A society built on those adaptations prizes endurance over empathy, competition over care. That's the water we swim in. It takes conscious effort to see it, and even greater effort to swim against it.

Guns Abroad, Fractures at Home

In America, trauma is not only personal—it is systemic. We are the world's largest supplier of arms and ammunition, exporting war machines as if they were symbols of national pride. At home, we have dismantled the family in service of the corporate workforce. Motherhood is rarely honored unless it is paired with a career, and children are left to find communion in peer groups shaped more by corporate advertising than by family or community. Screens have become teachers, and consumerism has replaced belonging.

We were told these systems existed to serve us, but they have only taught us how to serve them. We have fed them our time, our attention, our creativity—until even our inner lives are mined for profit.

Veterans return from wars with uniforms and guns into a war they can't name, but they know is there. It is quieter, more insidious— fought not with bullets but with debt, distraction, and despair. We are told this is peace, yet it demands our attention, our labor, our souls. What we refuse to face becomes our collective shadow, and the shadow thrives when people confuse numbness for peace.

The destruction of family and the proliferation of weapons are two sides of the same wound. Both elevate domination over connection. Both glorify survival while neglecting nurture. Both leave us restless, armored, unable to truly belong.

Shadow Projected, Mass Enchanted

We are told this is freedom. That is the trick. We are taught to see the cage as proof of our worth, to confuse captivity with accomplishment. Like prisoners in Plato's cave, we mistake the shadows on the wall for reality—because we have never been allowed to see the fire casting them. But once you glimpse it, the illusion cannot hold. You begin to understand that the system is not designed to free you. It is designed to keep you believing you are free.

And while it keeps us chasing those shadows, it keeps us fighting each other. We are already in a kind of civil war—though not the kind fought with rifles and flags. It is a war for our minds, for our attention, for control of our labor. They have turned us against each other—red against blue, conservative against liberal, donkeys against elephants—so that we never look up at the hands pulling all the strings. Our tribal instincts, once meant to protect us, have been hijacked to keep us divided.

Carl Jung warned that when people lose their sense of personal responsibility inside the mass, they become susceptible to projecting their shadow onto others, which fuels social hatred, scapegoating, and totalitarian movements (Jung, 1957). And in *Psychology and Religion* (1938), he wrote: The individual who wishes to have an answer to the problem of evil has need, first and foremost, of self-knowledge… The individual who is unconscious of himself acts in a blind, instinctive way and is, in addition, fooled by all collective suggestions. (Jung, 1938).

The Quiet War After War

This is the war veterans come home and feel but cannot name. It is quieter than gunfire but no less deadly. It is fought in headlines and hashtags, in algorithms that reward outrage and erase nuance, in workplaces that demand our obedience while promising freedom. It plays on the unacknowledged fears buried in what Jung called the shadow, and magnifies them across entire populations until neighbors and family members become enemies. It is not fought over land. It is fought over people's minds, and the endless extraction of their lives.

And you cannot escape it alone. You escape it by replacing it. Not with slogans or rage, but with something older and stronger: families who stand by one another, neighbors who feed and clothe each other, communities that raise children and grow food and care for their own. Cultures that do not ask what they can extract, but what they can protect. This is radical responsibility. It is harder than rebellion and quieter than protest, but it is the only way out. We will not be free until we make a culture that does not need our suffering to survive.

The machine is not made of steel. It is made of people. Real people who breathe and bleed just like you—who sell poison and bombs and call it food and freedom, then go home to their guarded private estates and feed their own children from organic farms. They build systems that flood our communities with chemicals and digital screens, then shield their children with tutors and clean air. They profit from war while sheltering their own sons from battle, and profit from illness while guarding their daughters from harm. To the public they sell chaos, and to their own they provide safety.

This is why the machine endures: because it does not care what it destroys, only that its own survive.

Tools or Chains

Artificial intelligence is not an alien mind; it's a mirror—polished by capital and trained on the fragments of ourselves we left across the digital world. It does not awaken; it predicts. And it will amplify whatever we feed it: our fears, our appetites, our attention.

So the fork is simple. Used with conscience, AI can hand us back hours, lower the heat of busywork, and help neighbors coordinate food, care, learning, and craft. Used without it, it will strip-mine attention, automate obedience, and tighten the old chains with new efficiency. A plow in the garden—or a lock on the gate.

What decides the outcome isn't the code; it's the culture behind it. If we want these systems to till the soil, we have to be gardeners first. That means limits over frictionless growth, transparency over capture, human judgment over automated punishment, and tools that serve households and neighborhoods before empires and markets. Feed the machine what you mean to multiply—or refuse it your life altogether.

Leaving the Cave

There is no switch to flip. There is only the slow, stubborn act of reclaiming your life from the systems that taught you to burn yourself down. They survive on your belief that you are nothing without them—that if you stop grinding, you will vanish. But that is the first lie. You are not what you produce. The way out is not rebellion or exile. It is choosing, day by day, to stop feeding them pieces of your soul. It is giving your time back to what makes you alive instead of what makes you useful. It is protecting your hours the way you would protect your child. It is saying no when the world demands you prove your worth in exhaustion.

This is how people leave the cave: they start to see their own light again. They walk slowly, blinking, toward the things that make them feel whole—connection, craft, care, nature, silence. At first the darkness calls them back, whispering of lost status and slipping security. But if they keep walking, they discover what the cave-dwellers never see: that life outside is still hard, but it is finally theirs. These systems cannot survive people who no longer measure themselves by them. That is the quiet revolution. You do not need to burn the cave down. You only need to stop mistaking its shadows for sunlight.

To the young people who may read this, I say: do not inherit the wars of your fathers without question. You do not need to offer your lives on the altar of endless conflict. You can choose another way. You can choose peace. It will not be the easy path—the world will call you naïve—but it takes profound courage to break the cycle and protect what gives life. Even the prophets once dreamed of a day when we would beat our swords into plowshares and learn war no more. That dream can begin with you.

We will not win by tearing the old world down, only by starving it of our obedience. The systems that feed on us cannot be reformed; they can only be abandoned. And that begins when even one person chooses to stop living as fuel. When one man stops measuring his worth in hours burned. When one woman refuses to trade her soul for survival. When one family becomes a refuge instead of a cog.

If enough of us do this—if enough of us build lives rooted in care, craft, and courage—the old world will wither for lack of what it needs most: our belief in it. That is how the war ends. Not with conquest, but with refusal. Not by fire, but by walking away from the furnace until it goes cold.

In Homer's *Odyssey*, even after Odysseus' return, vengeance threatened to ignite another cycle of bloodshed. But Athena descended and commanded the people to stop: Make peace at once and end this war of iron. The epic does not close with another battle—it closes with peace.

That is where I will close, too. Like Odysseus, I have carried scars and ghosts home with me. But I have also carried a choice. And my choice is this: to lay down the iron, to build instead of destroying, to live as a warrior in the garden.

To starve the machine and feed the soul.
In a culture wounded by war, domination, and silence, my responsibility is to live differently. To choose peace—not just for myself, but as a way of breaking the cycle. That is how I carry the scars forward: not as weapons, but as seeds.

Peace will not be given to us; it will grow where we dare to tend it.
And what we choose to tend, will outlive what we were taught to fear.

References

Butler, S. D. (1935/2003). *War is a racket.* Los Angeles, CA: Feral House.

Davidson, R. J., & Lutz, A. (2008). Buddha's brain: Neuroplasticity and meditation. *IEEE Signal Processing Magazine, 25*(1), 176–174. https://doi.org/10.1109/MSP.2008.4431873

Felitti, V. J., Anda, R. F., Nordenberg, D., Williamson, D. F., Spitz, A. M., Edwards, V., … Marks, J. S. (1998). Relationship of childhood abuse and household dysfunction to many of the leading causes of death in adults: The Adverse Childhood Experiences (ACE) Study. *American Journal of Preventive Medicine, 14*(4), 245–258. https://doi.org/10.1016/S0749-3797(98)00017-8

Gladwell, M. (2019). *Talking to strangers: What we should know about the people we don't know.* New York, NY: Little, Brown and Company.

Judith, A. (1996). *Eastern body, Western mind: Psychology and the chakra system as a path to the self.* Berkeley, CA: Celestial Arts.

Jung, C. G. (1938). *Psychology and religion* (R. F. C. Hull, Trans.). Princeton, NJ: Princeton University Press.

Jung, C. G. (1953). *Collected works of C. G. Jung, Volume 9 (Part 1): Archetypes and the collective unconscious* (R. F. C. Hull, Trans.). Princeton, NJ: Princeton University Press.

Jung, C. G. (1957). *The undiscovered self* (R. F. C. Hull, Trans.). Princeton, NJ: Princeton University Press.

Kaplan, S. (1995). The restorative benefits of nature: Toward an integrative framework. *Journal of Environmental Psychology, 15*(3), 169–182. https://doi.org/10.1016/0272-4944(95)90001-2

Levine, P. A. (1997/2010). *Waking the tiger: Healing trauma.* Berkeley, CA: North Atlantic Books.

Lipov, E. G., Rolain, H., & Neufeld, T. (2025). Treating post-traumatic stress disorder in Canadian Special Operation Forces Command with ketamine plus cervical sympathetic blockade. *Military Medicine.* Advance online publication. https://doi.org/10.1093/milmed/usae193

Litz, B. T., Stein, N., Delaney, E., Lebowitz, L., Nash, W. P., Silva, C., & Maguen, S. (2009). Moral injury and moral repair in war veterans: A preliminary model and intervention strategy. *Clinical Psychology Review, 29*(8), 695–706. https://doi.org/10.1016/j.cpr.2009.07.003

Malchiodi, C. A. (2007). *The art therapy sourcebook* (2nd ed.). New York, NY: McGraw-Hill.

Mason, J. W., Wang, S., Yehuda, R., Riney, S., Charney, D. S., & Southwick, S. M. (2001). Psychogenic lowering of urinary cortisol levels linked to increased emotional numbing and a shame-depressive syndrome in combat-related PTSD. *Psychosomatic Medicine, 63*(3), 387–401. https://doi.org/10.1097/00006842-200105000-00004

Mason, J. W., Wang, S., Yehuda, R., Lubin, H., Johnson, E. O., Southwick, S. M., & Charney, D. S. (2001). Marked lability in urinary cortisol levels in subgroups of combat veterans with posttraumatic stress disorder. *American Journal of Psychiatry, 158*(9), 1485–1491. https://doi.org/10.1176/appi.ajp.158.9.1485

Maté, G. (2010). *In the realm of hungry ghosts: Close encounters with addiction.* Berkeley, CA: North Atlantic Books.

Pacella, M. L., Hruska, B., & Delahanty, D. L. (2013). The physical health consequences of PTSD and PTSD symptoms: A meta-analytic review.

Journal of Anxiety Disorders, 27(1), 33–46.
https://doi.org/10.1016/j.janxdis.2012.08.004

Shay, J. (1994). *Achilles in Vietnam: Combat trauma and the undoing of character.* New York, NY: Scribner.

Shay, J. (2002). *Odysseus in America: Combat trauma and the trials of homecoming.* New York, NY: Scribner.

Teicher, M. H., Andersen, S. L., Polcari, A., Anderson, C. M., Navalta, C. P., & Kim, D. M. (2003). The neurobiological consequences of early stress and childhood maltreatment. *Neuroscience & Biobehavioral Reviews, 27*(1–2), 33–44. https://doi.org/10.1016/S0149-7634(03)00007-1

Ulrich, R. S. (1984). View through a window may influence recovery from surgery. *Science, 224*(4647), 420–421.
https://doi.org/10.1126/science.6143402

van der Kolk, B. A. (2014). *The body keeps the score: Brain, mind, and body in the healing of trauma.* New York, NY: Viking.

Yehuda, R., & Lehrner, A. (2018). Intergenerational transmission of trauma effects: Putative role of epigenetic mechanisms. *World Psychiatry, 17*(3), 243–257. https://doi.org/10.1002/wps.20568

Acknowledgment
For Grandma Jacks, who taught me to read before the world taught me to fight. The sound of her voice over a children's book was my first experience of peace.

And to every art teacher I ever had — thank you for giving me a language when I couldn't find the words. You showed me that making is another way of praying, and that creation is always an act of courage.

About the Author

Anthony Jacks is a U.S. Marine veteran, photographer, and multidisciplinary artist from Reno, Nevada. His work explores themes of transition, time, and healing through images and stories that blur the line between war and home, body and spirit, memory and light.

War Child is his first book — a testament to the endurance of love, the cost of forgetting, and the strange laughter that sometimes saves us when nothing else can.

Learn more or see his art at ajmakesart.com

Photo, Dean Burton.

www.ingramcontent.com/pod-product-compliance
Lightning Source LLC
Chambersburg PA
CBHW062059080426
42734CB00012B/2695